USDA

United States
Department of
Agriculture

Forest Service

Pacific Southwest
Research Station

General Technical
Report

PSW-GTR-230
September 2010

Central Florida Community Tree Guide

Benefits, Costs, and Strategic Planting

Paula J. Peper, E. Gregory McPherson, James R. Simpson,
Shannon N. Albers, and Qingfu Xiao

Authors

Paula J. Peper is an ecologist, **E. Gregory McPherson** is a research forester, **James R. Simpson** is a forest meteorologist, and **Shannon N. Albers** is a biological science technician, U.S. Department of Agriculture, Forest Service, Pacific Southwest Research Station, Center for Urban Forest Research, 1731 Research Park Dr., Davis, CA 95618; **Qingfu Xiao** is a research hydrologist, Department of Land, Air, and Water Resources, University of California, Davis, One Shields Ave., Davis, CA 95616.

Central Florida Community Tree Guide: Benefits, Costs, and Strategic Planting

Paula J. Peper, E. Gregory McPherson, James R. Simpson, Shannon N. Albers, and Qingfu Xiao

U.S. Department of Agriculture, Forest Service
Pacific Southwest Research Station
Albany, California
General Technical Report PSW-GTR-230
September 2010

This work was sponsored by the U.S. Department of Agriculture, Forest Service, State and Private Forestry, Urban and Community Forestry Program; the Florida Division of Forestry, Urban and Community Forestry; and the City of Orlando Families, Parks, and Recreation Department, Orlando Parks Division.

Abstract

Peper, Paula J.; McPherson, E. Gregory; Simpson, James R.; Albers, Shannon N.; Xiao, Qingfu 2010. Central Florida community tree guide: benefits, costs, and strategic planting. Gen. Tech. Rep. PSW-GTR-230. Albany, CA: U.S. Department of Agriculture, Forest Service, Pacific Southwest Research Station. 118 p.

Trees make our cities more attractive and provide many ecosystem services, including air quality improvement, energy conservation, stormwater interception, and atmospheric carbon dioxide reduction. These benefits must be weighed against the costs of maintaining trees, including planting, pruning, irrigation, administration, pest control, liability, cleanup, and removal. We present benefits and costs for representative small, medium, and large broadleaf trees and a conifer in the Central Florida region derived from models based on research carried out in Orlando, Florida. Average annual net benefits increase with tree size and differ based on location: $1 (public) to $10 (yard) for a small tree, $32 (public) to $51 (yard) for a medium tree, $96 (public) to $123 (yard) for a large tree; $7 (public) to $9 (yard) for a conifer. Two hypothetical examples of planting projects are described to illustrate how the data in this guide can be adapted to local uses, and guidelines for maximizing benefits and reducing costs are given.

Keywords: Ecosystem services, Central Florida region, urban forestry, benefit-cost analysis.

In the Central Florida region, trees play an environmental, cultural, and historical role in communities. Here grand old oaks grace a residential street in downtown Orlando.

Summary

Trees provide many valuable ecosystem services: they reduce energy consumption, they trap and filter stormwater, they help clean the air by intercepting air pollutants, and they help in the fight against global climate change by sequestering carbon dioxide (CO_2). At the same time, they provide a wide array of aesthetic, social, economic, and health benefits that are less tangible.

Benefits and costs quantified

This report quantifies benefits and costs for representative small, medium, and large broadleaf trees and a conifer in the Central Florida region: the species chosen as representative are the common crapemyrtle, Southern magnolia, live oak, and slash pine (see "Common and Scientific Names" section). The analysis describes "yard trees" (those planted in residential sites) and "public trees" (those planted on streets or in parks). Benefits are calculated based on tree growth curves and numerical models that consider regional climate, building characteristics, air pollutant concentrations, and prices. Tree care costs and mortality rates are based on results from a survey of municipal and commercial arborists. We assume a 60-percent survival rate over a 40-year timeframe.

The measurements used in modeling environmental and other benefits of trees are based on research carried out in Orlando, Florida. Given the Central Florida region's large geographical area, this approach provides general approximations based on some necessary assumptions that serve as a starting point for more specific local calculations. It is a general accounting of benefits and costs that can be easily adapted and adjusted for local tree planting projects. Two examples are provided that illustrate how to adjust benefits and costs to reflect different aspects of local planting projects.

Average annual benefits

Large trees provide the most benefits. Average annual benefits over 40 years increase with mature tree size and differ based on tree location. Except for conifers, the lowest values are for public trees and the highest values are for yard trees on the western side of houses. Benefits range as follows:

- $23 to $30 for a small tree (24 ft tall 40 years after planting)
- $59 to $74 for a medium tree (46 ft tall 40 years after planting)
- $127 to $149 for a large tree (56 ft tall 40 years after planting)
- $32 to $34 for a conifer (67 ft tall 40 years after planting)

Benefits associated with reduced levels of stormwater runoff and increased property values account for the largest proportion of total benefits in this region. Energy savings, reduced levels of air pollutants and CO_2 in the air are the next most important benefits.

Energy conservation benefits differ with tree location as well as size. Trees located opposite west-facing walls provide the greatest net cooling energy savings. Reducing energy needs reduces CO_2 emissions and thereby reduces atmospheric CO_2. Similarly, energy savings that reduce demand from powerplants account for important reductions in gases that produce ozone, a major component of smog.

The benefits of trees are offset by the costs of caring for them. Based on our surveys of municipal and commercial arborists, the average annual cost for tree care over 40 years ranges from $20 to $31 per tree. (Values below are for yard and public trees, respectively.)

- $20 and $22 for a small tree
- $23 and $27 for a medium tree
- $25 and $31 for a large tree
- $23 and $27 for a conifer

Planting costs, annualized over 40 years, are the greatest expense for yard trees ($11 per tree per year); planting costs for public trees are significantly lower ($6 per tree per year). For public trees, pruning ($7 to $11 per tree per year) and removal and disposal expenses ($4 to $6 per tree per year) are the greatest costs. Public trees also incur administrative costs, including inspections ($2 to $4 per tree per year).

Average annual net benefits (benefits minus costs) per tree for a 40-year period are as follows:

- $1 for a small public tree to $10 for a small yard tree on the west side of a house
- $32 for a medium public tree to $51 for a medium yard tree on the west side of a house
- $96 for a large public tree to $123 for a large yard tree on the west side of a house
- $7 for a public conifer to $9 for a yard conifer in a windbreak

Environmental benefits alone, including energy savings, stormwater runoff reduction, improved air quality, and reduced atmospheric CO_2, are greater than tree care costs for medium and large trees.

Net benefits for a yard tree opposite a west wall and a public tree are substantial when summed over the entire 40-year period:

- $403 (yard) and $23 (public) for a small tree
- $2,039 (yard) and $1,266 (public) for a medium tree
- $4,939 (yard) and $3,859 (public) for a large tree
- $344 (yard) and $296 (public) for a conifer

Costs

Average annual net benefits

Net benefits summed over 40 years

Private trees produce higher net benefits than public trees. Our survey results indicate that this is primarily due to higher maintenance costs for street and park trees. The standard of care is often higher for public trees because municipalities need to manage risk, maintain required clearances for pedestrians and vehicles, remove tree debris after hurricanes, and repair damage to sidewalks and curbing caused by tree roots.

To demonstrate ways that communities can adapt the information in this report to their needs, examples of two fictional cities interested in improving their urban forest have been created. The benefits and costs of different planting projects are determined. In the hypothetical city of Hurston Park, net benefits and benefit-cost ratios (BCRs; total benefits divided by costs) are calculated for a planting of 1,000 trees (2-in caliper) assuming a cost of $225 per tree, 40 percent mortality rate, and 40-year analysis. Total benefits are $4.4 million, total costs are about $1.1 million, and net benefits are $3.3 million ($83.66 per tree per year). The BCR is 4.09:1, indicating that $4.09 is returned for every $1 invested. The net benefits and BCRs (in parentheses) by mature tree size are:

- $4,461 (1.10:1) for 50 common crapemyrtle trees
- $230,799 (2.48:1) for 150 southern magnolia trees
- $3.1 million (4.97:1) for 700 live oaks
- $36,858 (1.35:1) for 100 slash pines

Increased property values reflecting aesthetic and other benefits of trees (52 percent) made up the largest share, and reduced stormwater runoff accounted for another 36 percent. Reduced energy (8 percent), air quality improvement (3 percent), and atmospheric CO_2 reduction (1 percent) make up the remaining benefits.

In the fictional city of Marcusville, long-term planting and tree care costs and benefits were compared to determine if current fashion for planting small flowering trees instead of the large stately trees that were once standard is substantially affecting the level of benefits residents are receiving. Over a 40-year period, the net benefits are:

- $11 for a small tree
- $1,205 for a medium tree
- $3,675 for a large tree

Based on this analysis, the city of Marcusville decided to strengthen its tree ordinance, requiring developers to plant large-growing trees wherever feasible and to create tree shade plans that show how they will achieve 50-percent shade over streets, sidewalks, and parking lots within 15 years of development.

Contents

The green infrastructure is a significant component of communities in the Central Florida region. This is one of the canals joining the chain of lakes in Winter Park, Florida.

Chapter 1. Introduction

The Central Florida Region

From small seashore towns dotting the east and west coasts to the city of Orlando, one of the world's primary tourist destinations, the Central Florida region (fig. 1) is a study in contrasts. Communities range from small, rural towns reminiscent of the Deep South to the sprawling, modern metropolitan areas surrounding Tampa, St. Petersburg, and Orlando. Home to over 8 million people, the region extends from Daytona Beach and Port St. Lucie on the east coast, through Orlando, Okeechobee and LaBelle, to Cape Coral, and Florida's "Suncoast" cities, Tampa and Clearwater. The warm climate has attracted both national and international immigration, making it one of the most culturally diverse areas in the Nation (U.S. Government 2010).

Figure 1—The Central Florida region is shown in dark gray. Reference cities for the Central Florida and other nearby regions are indicated with large circles. (Illustration courtesy of USDA Forest Service, PSW, Center for Urban Forest Research.)

Geographic scope of the Central Florida region

The **climate**[1] of this region is subtropical and corresponds to Sunset climate zone 26 (Brenzel 2001) and USDA hardiness zones 9 and 10, and is characterized by humid, warm to hot temperatures throughout the year. Thunderstorms are plentiful and rain heaviest in summer and early fall, averaging between 50 and 60 in of rain each year. Precipitation in coastal areas tends toward the higher end of this scale with inland areas receiving up to 10 in less annually. Average high temperatures range from the low 90s in July to the low 70s in January. Average low temperatures range from the high 40s in January to the low 70s in August. Hurricane season runs from June through November. Although communities in the state's interior do not usually experience wind and flood damage to the extent that coastal communities do, there are years where property damage is extensive. In 2004, for example, Orlando suffered the loss of an estimated 20,000 public and private trees when three hurricanes tore through the city.

As the communities of the Central Florida region continue to grow and change during the coming decades, growing and sustaining healthy **community forests** is integral to the quality of life that residents experience. The urban forest is a distinctive feature of the landscape that protects us from the elements, cleans the water we drink and the air we breathe, and forms a connection to earlier generations who planted and tended the trees.

Central Florida communities can derive many benefits from community forests

The role of urban forests in enhancing the environment, increasing community attractiveness and livability, and fostering civic pride takes on greater significance as communities strive to balance economic growth with environmental quality and social well-being. The simple act of planting trees provides opportunities to connect residents with nature and with each other (fig. 2). Neighborhood tree plantings and stewardship projects stimulate investment by local citizens, businesses, and governments for the betterment of their communities. Community forests bring opportunity for economic renewal, combating development woes, and increasing the quality of life for community residents.

Quality of life improves with trees

Central Florida communities can promote energy efficiency through tree planting and stewardship programs that strategically locate trees to save energy and minimize conflicts with urban infrastructure. The same trees can provide additional benefits by reducing stormwater runoff; improving local air, soil, and water quality; reducing atmospheric carbon dioxide (CO_2); providing wildlife habitat; increasing property values; slowing vehicular traffic; enhancing community attractiveness and investment; and promoting human health and well-being.

---

[1] Words in bold are defined in the glossary.

Figure 2—Tree planting and stewardship programs provide opportunities for local residents to work together to build better communities.

This guide builds upon studies by the U.S. Department of Agriculture, Forest Service, in Chicago and Sacramento (McPherson et al. 1994, 1997), and other regional tree guides from the Pacific Southwest Research Station (McPherson et al. 1999a, 1999b, 2000, 2003, 2004, 2006a, 2006b, 2006c, 2007; Peper et al. 2009b; Vargas et al. 2007a, 2007b) to extend knowledge of urban forest benefits in the Central Florida region. The guide:

Scope defined

- Quantifies benefits of trees on a per-tree basis rather than on a **canopy cover** basis (it should not be used to estimate benefits for trees growing in forest stands).
- Describes management costs and benefits.
- Details benefits and costs for trees in parks, residential yards, and along streets.
- Illustrates how to use this information to estimate benefits and costs for local tree planting projects.

These guidelines are specific to the Central Florida region and are based on measurements and calculations from open-growing urban trees in this region.

Street, park, and shade trees are integral to urban communities. However, with municipal tree programs dependent on taxpayer-supported general funds, communities are forced to ask whether trees are worth the price to plant and care for over the long term, thus requiring urban forestry programs to demonstrate their cost-effectiveness (McPherson 1995). If tree plantings are proven to benefit

Audience and objectives

communities, then financial commitment to tree programs will be justified. Therefore, the objective of this tree guide is to identify and describe the benefits and costs of planting trees in Central Florida communities—providing a tool for municipal tree managers, arborists, and tree enthusiasts to increase public awareness and support for trees (Dwyer and Miller 1999).

This tree guide addresses a number of questions about the environmental and aesthetic benefits of community tree plantings in Central Florida communities:

What will this tree guide do?

- How can tree-planting programs improve environmental quality, conserve energy, and add value to communities?
- Where should residential yard and public trees be placed to maximize their benefits?
- How can conflicts between trees and power lines, sidewalks, and buildings be minimized?

Paula Peper

Trees in Central Florida communities enhance quality of life.

Chapter 2. Benefits and Costs of Urban and Community Forests

This chapter describes benefits and costs of public and privately managed trees. Ecosystem services and associated economic value of community forests are described. Expenditures related to tree care and management are assessed—a necessary process for creating cost-effective programs (Dwyer et al. 1992, Hudson 1983).

Benefits

Saving Energy

Energy is essential to maintain quality of life and sustain economic growth. Conserving energy with shade trees can reduce the need for building new powerplants. For example, while California was experiencing energy shortages in 2001, its 177 million city trees were providing shade and conserving energy. Annual savings to utilities were an estimated $500 million in wholesale electricity and generation purchases (McPherson and Simpson 2003). Planting 50 million more shade trees in strategic locations would provide savings equivalent to seven 100-MWh powerplants. The cost of reducing the peak load was $63 per kW, considerably less than the $150 per kW threshold amount that is deemed cost-effective for energy conservation measures by the California Energy Commission (see http://www.fs.fed.us/psw/programs/cufr/products/3/cufr_148.pdf). Like electric utilities throughout the country, utilities in the Central Florida region could invest in shade tree programs as a cost-effective energy conservation measure.

How trees work to save energy

Trees modify climate and conserve building energy use in three principal ways (fig. 3):

* Shading reduces the amount of heat absorbed and stored by built surfaces, including buildings and paved areas.
* **Evapotranspiration** converts liquid water to water vapor and thus cools the air by using solar energy that would otherwise result in heating of the air.
* Windspeed reduction reduces the infiltration of outside air into interior spaces, especially where conductivity is relatively high (e.g., glass windows) (Simpson 1998).

Trees and other vegetation on individual building sites may lower air temperatures 5 °F compared with sites outside the **greenspace**. At larger scales (6 mi²), temperature differences of more than 9 °F have been observed between city centers

Figure 3—Trees save energy for cooling by shading buildings and lowering summertime temperatures. (Drawing by Mike Thomas.)

Trees lower temperatures

and more vegetated suburban areas (Akbari et al. 1992). These "hot spots" in cities are called **urban heat islands**. A recent study for New York City compared trees, living roofs, and light surfaces, finding that curbside tree planting was the most effective heat island mitigation strategy (Rosenzweig et al. 2006).

For individual buildings, strategically placed trees can increase energy efficiency. Because the sun is low in the east and west for several hours each day, trees that shade these walls in particular will help keep buildings cool.

Trees provide greater energy savings in the Central Florida region than in milder climate regions because they can have cooling effects year round. In Miami, for example, trees were found to produce substantial cooling savings for an energy-efficient two-story wood-frame house (McPherson et al. 1993). A typical energy-efficient house with air conditioning requires about $546 each year for cooling. A computer simulation demonstrated that three 25-ft-tall trees—two on the west side of the house and one on the east—would save $150 each year for cooling, a 28-percent reduction.

A recent study on tree shade and energy savings in Alabama showed that for every 10 percent shade coverage of a home, there was a summertime electricity reduction of 1.29 kWh per day. Conversely, for every 10 percent increase in average shade falling on a residential structure during winter, electricity use increased by 1.74 kWh per day, illustrating the importance of selecting deciduous, solar-friendly trees for shading homes (Pandit and Laband, in press).

Shading and **climate effects** of 68,211 municipal trees of Orlando reduced annual electricity used for air conditioning by 1,369 **MWh**, saving city residents approximately $445,451 in annual air conditioning (Peper et al. 2009b) or $6.53 per tree. The largest trees provide the largest benefits; the live oak (see "Common and Scientific Names" section), for example, accounted for 42 percent of the energy benefits although it represented only 25 percent of the population.

In Central Florida, there is ample opportunity to "retrofit" communities with more sustainable landscapes through strategic tree planting and care of existing trees.

Trees increase home energy efficiency and save money

Reducing Atmospheric Carbon Dioxide

Global temperatures have increased since the late 19th century, with major warming periods from 1910 to 1945 and from 1976 to the present (IPCC 2007). Human activities, primarily fossil-fuel consumption, are adding greenhouse gases to the atmosphere, and current research suggests that the recent increases in temperature can be attributed in large part to increases in greenhouse gases (IPCC 2007). Higher global temperatures are expected to have a number of adverse effects, including melting polar ice caps, which could raise sea level by 6 to 37 in by 2100 (Hamburg et al. 1997). With more than one-third of the world's population living in coastal areas (Cohen et al. 1997), the effects could be disastrous. Increasing frequency and duration of extreme weather events will continue to tax emergency management resources. Some plants and animals may become extinct as habitat becomes restricted (Hamburg et al. 1997).

Trees reduce CO_2

Urban forests have been recognized as important storage sites for carbon dioxide (CO_2), the primary greenhouse gas (Nowak and Crane 2002). At the same time, private markets dedicated to reducing CO_2 emissions by trading carbon credits are emerging (McHale et al. 2007). **Damage costs** of CO_2 emissions range from about $5 to $15 per **metric tonne** (Tol 2005). For every $18 spent on a tree planting project in Arizona, 1 ton of atmospheric CO_2 was reduced (McPherson and Simpson 1999). The Climate Action Reserve's (2010) *Urban Forest Project Protocol* provides guidance for tree planting and stewardship projects aimed at providing monetary resources for community forestry programs.

Urban forests can reduce atmospheric CO_2 in two ways (fig. 4):

- Trees directly sequester CO_2 in their stems, leaves, and roots while they grow.
- Trees near buildings can reduce the demand for air conditioning, thereby reducing emissions associated with power production.

Figure 4—Trees sequester carbon dioxide (CO_2) as they grow and indirectly reduce CO_2 emissions from powerplants through energy conservation. At the same time, CO_2 is released through decomposition and tree care activities that involve fossil-fuel consumption. (Drawing by Mike Thomas.)

Some tree-related activities release CO$_2$

On the other hand, vehicles, chain saws, chippers, and other equipment release CO_2 during the process of planting and maintaining trees. And eventually, all trees die, and most of the CO_2 that has accumulated in their biomass is released into the atmosphere through burning or decomposition. The rate of release into the atmosphere depends on if and how the wood is reused. For instance, recycling of urban wood waste into products such as furniture can delay the rate of decomposition compared to its reuse as mulch.

Typically, CO_2 released owing to tree planting, maintenance, and other program-related activities is about 2 to 8 percent of annual CO_2 reductions obtained through **sequestration** and **reduced powerplant emissions** (McPherson and Simpson 1999). To provide a complete picture of atmospheric CO_2 reductions from tree plantings, it is important to consider CO_2 released into the atmosphere through tree planting and tree maintenance operations, as well as decomposition of wood from pruned or dead trees.

Regional variations in climate and the mix of fuels that produce energy to cool buildings influence potential CO_2 emission reductions. The average emission rate in Orlando, Florida, is 2,079 lb of CO_2 per MWh (US EPA 2006b), a high value, because 97.9 percent of Orlando's power is generated from oil. The state of Florida, on the other hand, derives its energy from less CO_2-intensive sources—a mix of coal, oil, natural gas, and nuclear power—and therefore has an average emission of 1,327 lbs of CO_2 per MWh, which is close to the national average of 1,363 lb of CO_2 per MWh (US EPA 2006b). Cities in the Central Florida region with relatively high CO_2 emission rates will see greater benefits from reduced energy demand relative to other areas with lower emissions rates. Nevertheless, tree planting programs targeted to maximize energy savings will provide climate protection dividends throughout the Central Florida region.

A study of the municipal trees of Orlando found that the 68,211 trees in the inventory sequester about 11,531 tons of CO_2 (Peper et al. 2009b) annually and, by reducing energy use, reduce the production of CO_2 at the powerplant by 3,431 tons. Approximately 1,380 tons of CO_2 is released from decaying trees and during maintenance, with a positive net reduction in CO_2 from trees of 13,582 tons.

A recent study of Tampa's urban forest estimated that the amount of carbon sequestered or removed from the atmosphere by the city's 7.8 million trees was 46,525 tons in 2007, valued conservatively at $945,396 (Andreu et al. 2008).

A study in Chicago focused on the carbon sequestration benefit of residential tree canopy. Tree **canopy cover** in two residential neighborhoods was estimated to sequester on average 0.112 lb/ft^2, and pruning activities released 0.016 lb/ft^2 (Jo and McPherson 1995). Net annual carbon uptake was 0.096 lb/ft^2.

A comprehensive study of CO_2 reduction by Sacramento's urban forest found the region's 6 million trees offset 1.8 percent of the total CO_2 emitted annually as a byproduct of human activities (McPherson 1998). This savings could be substantially increased through strategic planting and long-term stewardship that maximize future energy savings from new tree plantings.

Since 1990, the Sacramento Tree Foundation, a nonprofit organization, has partnered with the Sacramento Municipal Utility District to plant trees for energy savings and atmospheric CO_2 reduction. Nearly 500,000 trees have been planted

Avoided CO_2 emissions

CO_2 reduction through community forestry

with the help of local residents. These trees are estimated to have offset CO_2 emissions by 807,394 t and provided 12,313 GWh of cooling energy savings and 3.54 MW of capacity savings (Sarkovich 2009).

Improving Air Quality

Trees improve air
quality

Approximately 159 million people live in areas where **ozone (O_3)** concentrations violate federal air quality standards. About 100 million people live in areas where dust and other small **particulate matter (PM_{10})** exceed levels for healthy air. Air pollution is a serious health threat to many city dwellers, contributing to asthma, coughing, headaches, respiratory and heart disease, and cancer (Smith 1990). Impaired health results in increased social costs for medical care, greater absenteeism, and reduced longevity. Short-term increases in O_3 concentrations have been statistically associated with increased mortality for 95 large U.S. cities (Bell et al. 2004). Impaired health results in increased social costs for medical care, greater absenteeism, and reduced longevity.

Recently, the U.S. Environmental Protection Agency recognized tree planting as a measure in state implementation plans for reducing O_3. Air quality management districts have funded tree planting projects to control particulate matter. These policy decisions are creating new opportunities to plant and care for trees as a method for controlling air pollution (Bond 2006, Hughes 2008, Luley and Bond 2002; for more information see www.treescleanair.org).

Urban forests provide a number of air quality benefits (fig. 5):

- They absorb gaseous pollutants (e.g., O_3, **nitrogen dioxide [NO_2]**, and **sulfur dioxide [SO_2]**) through leaf surfaces.
- They intercept PM_{10} (e.g., dust, ash, pollen, smoke).
- They release oxygen through **photosynthesis**.
- They reduce energy use, which reduces emissions of pollutants from powerplants, including NO_2, SO_2, PM_{10}, and volatile organic compounds (**VOCs**).
- They transpire water and shade surfaces, which lowers air temperatures, thereby reducing O_3 levels.

Trees may also adversely affect air quality. Most trees emit **biogenic volatile organic compounds** (BVOCs) such as isoprenes and monoterpenes that can contribute to O_3 formation. The contribution of BVOC emissions from city trees to O_3 formation depends on complex geographic and atmospheric interactions that have not been studied in most cities. Some complicating factors include variations with temperature and atmospheric levels of NO_2. As well, the O_3-forming potential

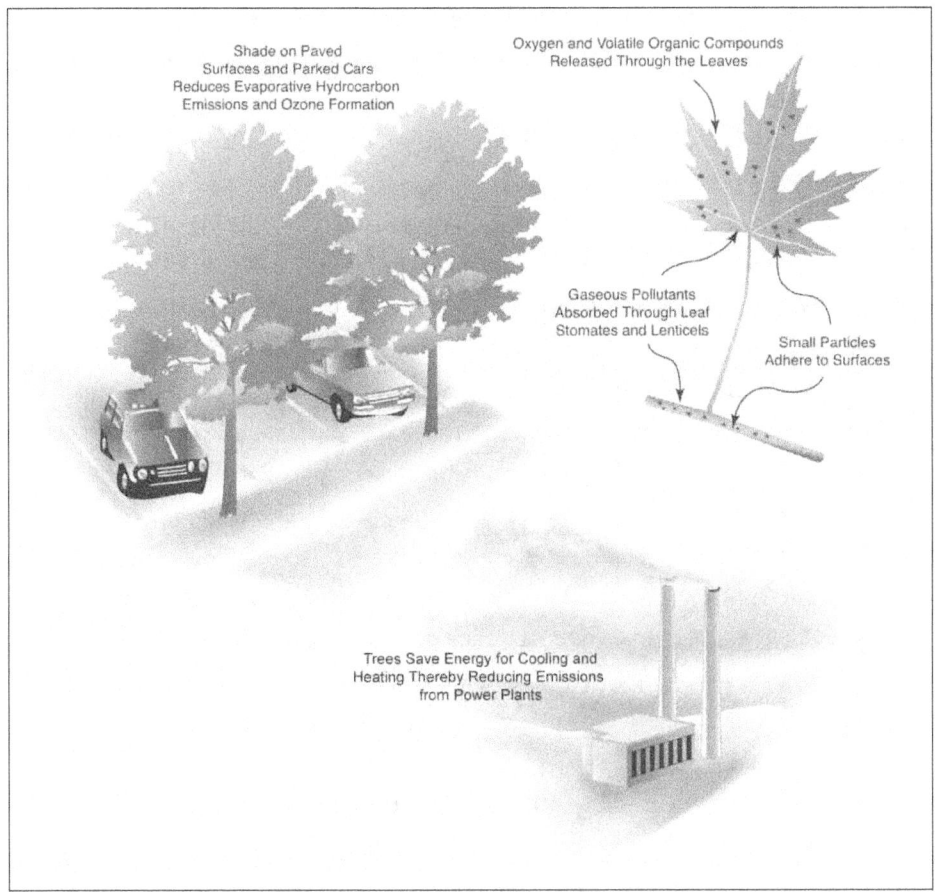

Figure 5—Trees absorb gaseous pollutants, retain particles on their surfaces, and release oxygen and volatile organic compounds. By cooling urban heat islands and shading parked cars, trees can reduce ozone formation. (Drawing by Mike Thomas.)

differs considerably for different tree species (Benjamin and Winer 1998). Genera having the greatest relative effect on increasing O_3 are sweetgum, blackgum, sycamore, poplar, and oak (Nowak 2000).

A computer simulation study for Atlanta suggested that it would be very difficult to meet EPA ozone standards in the region by using trees because of the high BVOC emissions from native pines and other vegetation (Chameides et al. 1988). Although removing trees reduced BVOC emissions, this effect was overwhelmed by increased hydrocarbon emissions from natural and **anthropogenic** sources owing to the increased air temperatures associated with tree removal (Cardelino and Chameides 1990). In the Los Angeles basin, increased planting of low BVOC-emitting tree species would reduce O_3 concentrations, whereas planting of medium and high emitters would increase overall O_3 concentrations (Taha 1996). A study in

Trees affect ozone formation

the Northeastern United States, however, found that species mix had no detectable effects on O_3 concentrations (Nowak et al. 2000). Although new trees increased BVOC emissions, ambient VOC emissions were so high that additional BVOCs had little effect on air quality. These potentially negative effects of trees on one kind of air pollution must be considered in light of their great benefit in other areas.

Trees absorb gaseous pollutants

Trees absorb gaseous pollutants through stomates, tiny openings in the leaves. Secondary methods of pollutant removal include adsorption of gases to plant surfaces and uptake through bark pores (lenticels). Once gases enter the leaf, they diffuse into intercellular spaces, where some react with inner leaf surfaces and others are absorbed by water films to form acids. Pollutants can damage plants by altering their metabolism and growth. At high concentrations, pollutants cause visible damage to leaves, such as spotting and bleaching (Costello and Jones 2003). Although they may pose health hazards to plants, pollutants such as nitrogenous gases can be sources of essential nutrients for trees.

Trees intercept particulate matter

Trees intercept small airborne particles. Some particles that are intercepted by a tree are absorbed, but most adhere to plant surfaces. Species with hairy or rough leaf, twig, and bark surfaces are efficient interceptors (Smith and Dochinger 1976). Intercepted particles are often resuspended to the atmosphere when wind blows the branches, and rain will wash some particulates off plant surfaces. The ultimate fate of these pollutants depends on whether they fall onto paved surfaces and enter the stormwater system, or fall on pervious surfaces, where they are filtered in the soil.

Trees near buildings can reduce the demand for air conditioning, thereby reducing emissions of PM_{10}, SO_2, NO_2, and VOCs associated with electric power production, an effect that can be sizable. For example, a strategically located tree can save 100 kWh in electricity for cooling annually (McPherson and Simpson 1999, 2002, 2003). Assuming that this conserved electricity comes from a typical new coal-fired powerplant in the Central Florida region, the tree reduces emissions of SO_2 by 0.23 lb, NO_2 by 0.28 lb (US EPA 2006b), and PM_{10} by 0.1 lb (US EPA 1998). The same tree is responsible for conserving 60 gal of water in cooling towers and reducing CO_2 emissions by 204 lb.

Although air pollutants removed and avoided owing to energy savings from Orlando's municipal forest had substantial value ($203,645 annually), the releases of BVOCs reduced the net air-quality benefit to $115,237 (Peper et al. 2009b). The ability of trees to produce net air-quality benefits differed dramatically among species; those with low BVOC emissions produced significant benefits. Large-canopied trees with large **leaf surface areas** and low BVOC emissions produced the greatest benefits. Although live and laurel oak were classified as high emitters, their large amount of leaf surface area resulted in substantial net air quality benefits ($81,711 total) .

The urban forests in Jacksonville and Miami were estimated to remove 11,000 and 243 tons of air pollutants, a service valued at $60.8 and $1.4 million, respectively (Nowak et al. 2006). Removal of 1,380 tons of air pollutants by Tampa's urban forest was valued at $6.4 million (Andreu et al. 2009). Another study in Palm Beach County, Florida, assessed the damage done to the urban canopy by recent hurricanes and calculated the benefits lost. Between 2004 and 2006, the tree canopy of the urbanized parts of the county declined by 38 percent and thereby increased the level of air pollutants in the atmosphere by approximately 2.3 million pounds (American Forests 2007).

Trees in a Davis, California, parking lot were found to improve air quality by reducing air temperatures 1 to 3 °F (Scott et al. 1999). By shading asphalt surfaces and parked vehicles, trees reduce hydrocarbon emissions (VOCs) from gasoline that evaporates out of leaky fuel tanks and worn hoses) (fig. 6). These evaporative emissions are a principal component of smog, and parked vehicles are a primary source. In California, parking lot tree plantings can be funded as an air quality improvement measure because of the associated reductions in evaporative emissions.

Trees shade prevents evaporative hydrocarbon emissions

USDA Forest Service, PSW, Center for Urban Forest Research

Figure 6—Trees planted to shade parking areas can reduce hydrocarbon emissions and improve air quality.

Reducing Stormwater Runoff and Improving Hydrologic Function

Urban stormwater runoff is a major source of pollution entering wetlands, streams, lakes, and oceans. Healthy trees can reduce the amount of runoff and pollutants in receiving waters (Cappiella et al. 2005). This is important because federal law requires states and localities to control nonpoint-source pollution, such as runoff from pavements, buildings, and landscapes. Also, many older cities have combined sewer outflow systems, and during large rain events excess runoff can mix with raw sewage. Rainfall **interception** by trees can reduce the magnitude of this problem during large storms. Trees are mini-reservoirs, controlling runoff at the source, thereby reducing runoff volumes and erosion of watercourses, as well as delaying the onset of **peak flows**. Trees can reduce runoff in several ways (fig. 7):

- Leaves and branch surfaces intercept and store rainfall, thereby reducing runoff volumes and delaying the onset of peak flows.
- Roots increase the rate at which rainfall infiltrates soil by creating root channels. This increases the capacity of soil to store water, reducing overland flow.
- Tree canopies and litter reduce soil erosion by diminishing the impact of raindrops on barren surfaces.
- **Transpiration** through tree leaves reduces moisture levels in the soil, increasing the soil's capacity to store rainfall.

Trees reduce runoff

Rainfall that is stored temporarily on canopy leaf and bark surfaces is called intercepted rainfall. Intercepted water evaporates, drips from leaf surfaces, and flows down stem surfaces to the ground. Tree surface saturation generally occurs after 1 to 2 in of rain has fallen (Xiao et al. 2000). During large storm events, rainfall exceeds the amount that the tree **crown** can store, about 50 to 100 gal per tree. The interception benefit is the amount of rainfall that does not reach the ground because it evaporates from the crown. As a result, the volume of runoff is reduced and the time of peak flow is delayed. Trees protect water quality by substantially reducing runoff during small rainfall events that are responsible for most pollutant washoff into receiving water bodies. Therefore, urban forests generally produce more benefits through water quality protection than through flood control (Xiao et al. 1998, 2000).

The amount of rainfall trees intercept depends on the tree's architecture, rainfall patterns, and climate. Tree-crown characteristics that influence interception are the trunk, stem, surface areas, textures, area of gaps, period when leaves are present, and dimensions (e.g., tree height and diameter). Trees with coarse surfaces retain more rainfall than those with smooth surfaces. Large trees generally intercept

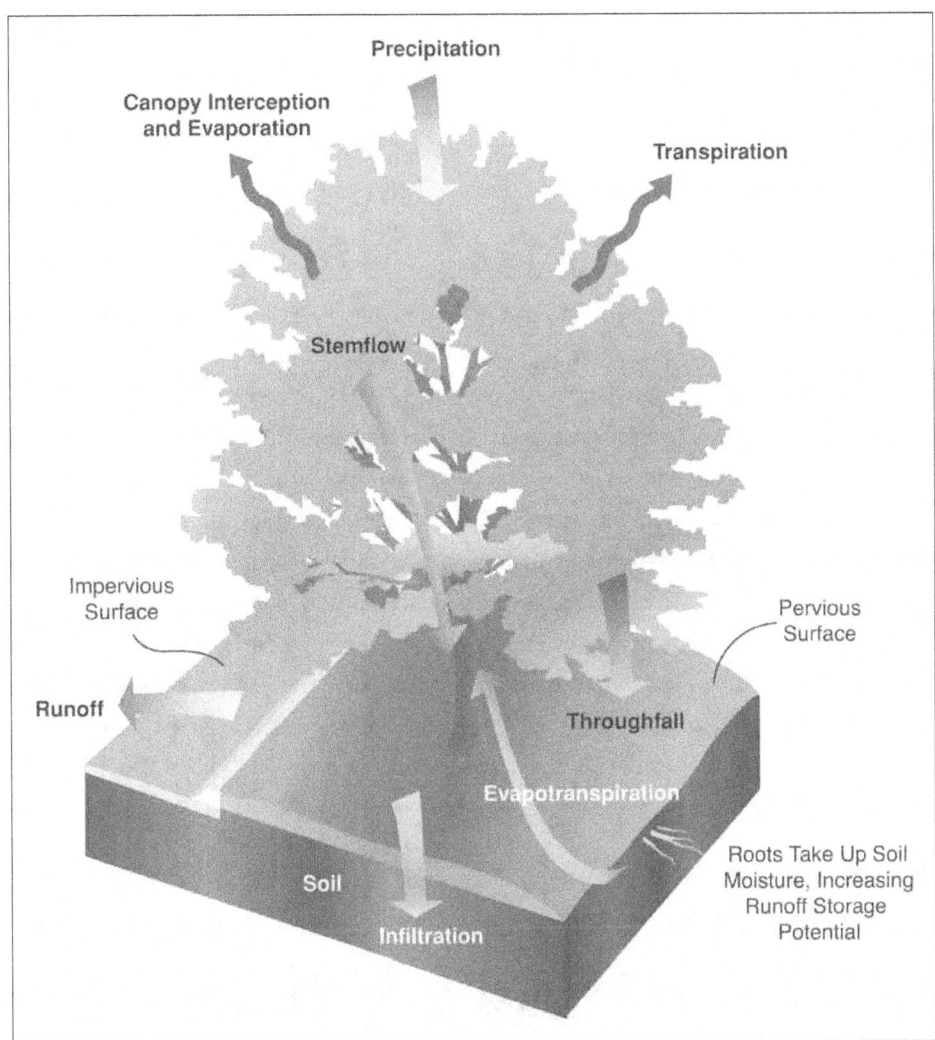

Figure 7—Trees intercept a portion of rainfall that evaporates and never reaches the ground. Some rainfall runs to the ground along branches and stems (stemflow), and some falls through gaps or drips off leaves and branches (throughfall). Transpiration increases soil moisture storage potential. (Drawing by Mike Thomas.)

more rainfall than small trees do because greater surface areas allow for greater evaporation rates. Tree crowns with few gaps reduce **throughfall** to the ground. Species that are in leaf when rainfall is plentiful are more effective than **deciduous** species that have dropped their leaves during the rainy season.

Studies in California that have simulated urban forest effects on stormwater runoff have reported reductions of 2 to 7 percent. Annual interception of rainfall by Sacramento's urban forest for the total urbanized area was only about 2 percent because of the winter rainfall pattern and scarcity of **evergreen** species (Xiao et al. 1998). However, average interception in canopied areas ranged from 6 to 13 percent

(150 gal per tree), similar to values reported for rural forests. Broadleaf evergreens and **conifers** intercept more rainfall than deciduous species in areas where rainfall is highest in fall, winter, or spring (Xiao and McPherson 2002). However, deciduous trees in Florida are in full leaf during peak precipitation months, June to November, and intercept a significant amount of rainfall.

In Orlando, Florida, the municipal forest reduced runoff by 284 million gallons annually (Peper et al. 2009b), valued at $851,291. Tree species with the highest rate of interception were laurel oak, live oak, and camphor. The American Forests (2007) study of Palm Beach County, Florida, found that the 38 percent decline in the urban forest canopy between 2004 and 2006 owing to hurricanes meant that an additional 1 billion gallons of stormwater had to be treated.

Urban forests can provide other hydrologic benefits, too. For example, when planted in conjunction with engineered soil around paved areas, trees can serve as mini stormwater reservoirs, capturing and filtering much more runoff than the trees alone. Tree plantations, nurseries, or landscapes can be irrigated with partially treated wastewater. Reused wastewater applied to urban forest lands can recharge aquifers, reduce stormwater-treatment loads, and create income through sales of nursery or wood products from the forests. Recycling urban wastewater into greenspace areas can be an economical means of treatment and disposal while at the same time providing other environmental benefits (USDA NRCS 2005).

Aesthetics and Other Benefits

Beautification

Trees provide a host of aesthetic, social, economic, and health benefits that should be included in any benefit-cost analysis. One of the most frequently cited reasons that people plant trees is for beautification. Trees add color, texture, line, and form to the landscape, softening the hard geometry that dominates built environments. Research on the aesthetic quality of residential streets has shown that street trees are the single strongest positive influence on scenic quality (Schroeder and Cannon 1983).

In surveys, consumers have shown greater preference for commercial street-scapes with trees. In contrast to areas without trees, people shop more often and longer in well-landscaped business districts. They are willing to pay more for parking and up to 12 percent more for goods and services (Wolf 2007).

Public safety benefits

Research in public housing complexes found that outdoor spaces with trees were used significantly more often than spaces without trees. By facilitating inter-actions among residents, trees can contribute to reduced levels of domestic violence, as well as foster safer and more sociable neighborhood environments (Sullivan and Kuo 1996).

Well-maintained trees increase the "curb appeal" of properties (fig. 8). Research documenting the increase in dollar value that can be attributed to trees is difficult to conduct and still in early stages, but some studies comparing sales prices of residential properties with different numbers of trees have suggested that people are willing to pay 3 to 7 percent more for properties with ample trees versus few or no trees. One of the most comprehensive studies of the influence of trees on home property values was based on actual sales prices in Athens, Georgia, and found that each large front-yard tree was associated with about a 1-percent increase in sales price (Anderson and Cordell 1988). A much greater value of 9 percent ($15,000) was determined in a U.S. Tax Court case for the loss of a large black oak on a property valued at $164,500 (Neely 1988). In Portland, Oregon, street trees added on average $7,020 to the sales price of a home ($297,115) (Donovan and Butry 2008).

Property value benefits

Scientific studies confirm that trees in cities provide social and psychological benefits. Humans derive substantial pleasure from trees, whether it is inspiration from their beauty, a spiritual connection, or a sense of meaning (Dwyer et al. 1992, Lewis 1996). After natural disasters, people often report a sense of loss if their community forest has been damaged (Hull 1992). Views of trees and nature from homes and offices provide restorative experiences that ease mental fatigue and help people to concentrate (Kaplan and Kaplan 1989). Desk workers with a view of nature report lower rates of sickness and greater satisfaction with their jobs compared to those having no visual connection to nature (Kaplan 1992).

Social and psychological benefits

Paula Peper

Figure 8—Trees beautify a neighborhood, increasing property values and creating a more sociable environment.

Trees provide important settings for recreation and relaxation in and near cities. The act of planting trees can have social value, as bonds between people and local groups often result.

The presence of trees in cities provides public health benefits and improves the well-being of those who live, work, and play in cities. Physical and emotional stress has both short-term and long-term effects. Prolonged stress can compromise the human immune system. A series of studies on human stress caused by general urban conditions and city driving show that views of nature reduce the stress response of both body and mind (Parsons et al. 1998). Urban green also appears to have an "immunization effect," in that people show less stress response if they have had a recent view of trees and vegetation. Hospitalized patients with views of nature and time spent outdoors need less medication, sleep better, have a better outlook, and recover more quickly than patients without connections to nature (Ulrich 1985).

Skin cancer is a particular concern in the sunny, low-latitude Central Florida region. By providing shade, trees reduce exposure to ultraviolet (UV) light, thereby lowering the risk of harmful effects from skin cancer and cataracts (Tretheway and Manthe 1999). In low-latitude regions like the Tropics, the ultraviolet protection factor provided by trees increases from approximately 2 under a 30-percent canopy cover to as much as 30 under a 90-percent canopy cover (Grant et al. 2002). Because early exposure to UV radiation is a risk factor for later development of skin cancer, planting trees around playgrounds, schools, day care centers, and ball fields can be especially valuable in helping reduce the risk of later-life cancers.

Certain environmental benefits from trees are more difficult to quantify than those previously described, but can be just as important. Noise can reach unhealthy levels in cities. Trucks, trains, and planes can produce noise that exceeds 100 decibels, twice the level at which noise becomes a health risk. Thick strips of vegetation in conjunction with landforms or solid barriers can reduce some highway noise and have a psychological effect (Cook 1978).

Numerous types of wildlife inhabit cities and are generally highly valued by residents. For example, older parks, cemeteries, and botanical gardens often contain a rich assemblage of wildlife. Remnant woodlands and **riparian habitats** within cities can connect a city to its surrounding bioregion (fig. 9). Wetlands, greenways (linear parks), and other greenspace can provide habitats that conserve **biodiversity** (Platt et al. 1994). Native plants are particularly valuable because they support wildlife. Also, regionally appropriate and native plant selections reduce potential resource inputs.

Urban forestry can provide jobs for both skilled and unskilled labor. Public service programs and grassroots-led urban and community forestry programs provide

Human health benefits

Wildlife habitat

Paula Peper

Figure 9—Natural areas within cities are refuges for wildlife and help connect city dwellers with their ecosystems. Shown here is one of many homes that border a multitude of lakes throughout Central Florida communities. These lakes provide habitat for birds, amphibians, alligators, and other wildlife.

horticultural training to volunteers across the United States. Also, urban and community forestry provides educational opportunities for residents who want to learn about nature through firsthand experience (McPherson and Mathis 1999). Local nonprofit tree groups and municipal volunteer programs often provide educational material and hands-on training in the care of trees and work with area schools.

Jobs and environmental education

Tree shade on streets can help offset the cost of managing pavement by protecting it from weathering. The asphalt paving on streets contains stone aggregate in an oil binder. Tree shade lowers the street surface temperature and reduces heating and volatilization of the binder (McPherson and Muchnick 2005). As a result, the aggregate remains protected for a longer period by the oil binder. When unprotected, vehicles loosen the aggregate, and much like sandpaper, the loose aggregate grinds down the pavement. Because most weathering of asphalt-concrete pavement occurs during the first 5 to 10 years when new street tree plantings provide little shade, this benefit mainly applies when older streets are resurfaced (fig. 10).

Costs

Planting and Maintaining Trees

The environmental, social, and economic benefits of urban and community forests come, of course, at a price. A national survey reported that communities in the Gulf Coast region spent an average of $0.98 per tree, in 1994, for street- and park-tree management (Tschantz and Sacamano 1994). This is the lowest amount reported compared with average expenditures in all other regions. Nationwide, the single largest expenditure was for tree pruning, followed by tree removal/disposal, and tree planting.

Figure 10—Although shade trees can be expensive to maintain, their shade can reduce the costs of resurfacing streets (McPherson and Muchnick 2005), promote pedestrian travel, and improve air quality directly through pollutant uptake and indirectly through reduced emissions of volatile organic compounds from cars.

Municipal costs of tree care

Our survey of **municipal foresters** in Central Florida indicates that on average they are spending about $22 to $31 per tree annually. Most of this amount is for pruning ($7 to $11 per tree) and removal and disposal ($4 to $6 per tree), and administration ($2 to 4 per tree). Other municipal departments incur costs for infrastructure repair and trip-and-fall claims resulting from root-buckled pavement that average to about $2 per tree depending on city policy.

Residential costs vary

Annual expenditures for tree management on private property have also not been well documented. Costs differ considerably, ranging from some commercial or residential properties that receive regular professional landscape service to others that are virtually "wild" and without maintenance. An analysis of data for Sacramento suggested that households typically spent about $5 to $10 annually per tree for pruning and pest and disease control (Summit and McPherson 1998). Our survey of commercial arborists in the Central Florida region indicated that expenditures typically exceed that amount, ranging from $20 to $25 per tree with less than half of residential trees receiving care. Expenditures are usually greatest for planting, pruning, and removal.

Conflicts With Urban Infrastructure

Like other cities across the United States, communities in the Central Florida region are spending millions of dollars each year to manage conflicts between trees and power lines, sidewalks, sewers, and other elements of the urban infrastructure. Orlando is currently spending over $15 per tree annually on sewer, sidewalk, curb, and gutter repair costs (Peper et al. 2009b). Although this amount exceeds the value of $11.22 per tree reported for 18 California cities (McPherson 2000), it also includes sewer repair costs not included in the California study.

In some cities, decreasing budgets are increasing the sidewalk-repair backlog and forcing cities to shift the costs of sidewalk repair to residents. This shift has significant impacts on residents in older areas, where large trees have outgrown small sites and infrastructure has deteriorated. It should be noted that trees are not always solely responsible for these problems. In older areas, in particular, sidewalks and curbs may have reached the end of their 20- to 25-year service life, or may have been poorly constructed in the first place (Sydnor et al. 2000).

Tree roots can damage sidewalks

Efforts to control the costs of these conflicts are having alarming effects on urban forests (Bernhardt and Swiecki 1993, Thompson and Ahern 2000):

- Cities are downsizing their urban forests by planting smaller trees. Although small trees are appropriate under power lines and in small planting sites, they are less effective than large trees at providing shade, absorbing air pollutants, and intercepting rainfall.

- Thousands of healthy urban trees are lost each year and their benefits forgone because of sidewalk damage, the second most common reason that street and park trees were removed.

- Most cities surveyed were removing more trees than they were planting. Residents forced to pay for sidewalk repairs may not want replacement trees.

Cost-effective strategies to retain benefits from large street trees while reducing costs associated with infrastructure conflicts are described in *Reducing Infrastructure Damage by Tree Roots* (Costello and Jones 2003). Matching the growth characteristics of trees to the conditions at the planting site is one important strategy. Other strategies include meandering sidewalks around trees, suspending sidewalks above tree roots, and replacing concrete sidewalks with recycled rubber sidewalks.

Tree roots can also damage old sewer lines that are cracked or otherwise susceptible to invasion (Randrup et al. 2001). Sewer repair companies estimate that sewer damage is minor until trees and sewers are over 30 years old, and roots from trees in yards are usually more of a problem than roots from trees in planter strips along streets. The latter assertion may be because the sewers are closer to the root zone as they enter houses than at the street. Repair costs typically range from $100 for sewer rodding (inserting a cleaning implement to temporarily remove roots) to $1,000 or more for sewer excavation and replacement.

Most communities sweep their streets regularly to reduce surface-runoff pollution entering local waterways. Street trees drop leaves, flowers, fruit, and branches year round that constitute a significant portion of debris collected from city streets. When leaves fall and rains begin, **tree litter** can clog sewers, dry wells, and other elements of flood-control systems. Costs include additional labor needed to remove leaves, and property damage caused by localized flooding.

In Central Florida communities, hurricanes contribute to higher than average cleanup costs. Debris production has ranged from 0.2 (Sanford, Florida) to 60.7 cubic yards (Gulf Breeze, Florida) per 100 ft of studied road segments (Escobedo et al. 2009). The smaller amount is associated with a city in interior Florida compared to the larger amount for a coastal community. Cost of removal and disposal averaged $21.50 per yard. The cost of tree cleanup from the three hurricanes during the 2004–2005 season was nearly $23 million. About 20,000 municipal trees were lost and many more damaged.

Large trees under power lines can be costly

The cost of addressing conflicts between trees and power lines is reflected in electric rates. Large trees under power lines require more frequent pruning than better-suited trees, which can make them appear less attractive (fig. 11). Frequent crown reduction reduces the benefits these trees could otherwise provide. Moreover, increased costs for pruning are passed on to customers.

USDA Forest Service, PSW, Center for Urban Forest Research

Figure 11—Large trees planted under power lines can require extensive pruning, which increases tree care costs and reduces the benefits of those trees, including their appearance.

Wood Salvage, Recycling, and Disposal

According to our survey, green waste recycling in Central Florida cities ranges from 0 percent to 100 percent. Some of those recycle 100 percent of their green waste from urban trees as mulch, compost, and firewood. Some powerplants will use this wood to generate electricity, thereby helping defray costs for hauling and grinding. Some cities, like St. Petersburg, Florida, pay recyclers as much as $24 per ton, but realize a $14 per ton savings compared to dumping the green waste in a landfill. Generally, the net costs of waste-wood disposal are less than 1 percent of total tree-care costs, and cities and contractors may break even. Hauling and recycling costs can be nearly offset by revenues from sales of mulch, milled lumber, and firewood. The cost of wood disposal may be higher depending on geographic location and the presence of exotic pests that require elaborate waste-wood disposal (Bratkovich 2001). Growing markets for urban wood products and biomass feedstock for biopower plants could turn this cost into a revenue source.

Recycling green waste may pay for itself

Chapter 3. Benefits and Costs of Community Forests in Central Florida Communities

This chapter presents estimated benefits and costs for trees planted in typical residential yards and public sites in Central Florida communities. Because benefits and costs differ with tree size, we report results for representative small, medium, and large broadleaf trees and for a representative conifer.

Estimates are initial approximations as some benefits and costs are intangible or difficult to quantify (e.g., impacts on psychological health, crime, and violence). Limited knowledge about physical processes at work and their interactions makes estimates imprecise (e.g., fate of air pollutants trapped by trees and then washed to the ground by rainfall). Tree growth and mortality rates are highly variable throughout the region. Benefits and costs also differ, depending on differences in climate, pollutant concentrations, maintenance practices, and other factors. Given the Central Florida region's diverse landscape, with different soils and types of community forestry programs, the approach used here provides first-order approximations. These findings can be used for general planning purposes, but should not be applied to estimate benefits produced by individual trees in the landscape. They provide a basis for decisions that set priorities and influence management direction, but are not suitable for determining whether a specific tree should be removed or retained (Maco and McPherson 2003).

Overview of Procedures

Approach

In this study, annual benefits and costs are estimated over a 40-year planning horizon for newly planted trees in three residential yard locations (about 27 ft from the east, south, and west of the residence) and a public streetside or park location. Henceforth, we refer to trees in these hypothetical locations as "yard" trees and "public" trees, respectively. Prices are assigned to each cost (e.g., planting, pruning, removal, irrigation, infrastructure repair, liability) and benefit (e.g., heating/cooling energy savings, air pollutant mitigation, stormwater runoff reduction, property value increase) through direct estimation and implied valuation of benefits as environmental externalities. This approach makes it possible to estimate the net benefits of plantings in "typical" locations using "typical" tree species. More information on data collection, modeling procedures, and assumptions can be found in appendix 3.

To account for differences in the mature size and growth of different tree species, we report results for three broadleaf trees—the small crapemyrtle, medium Southern magnolia, and large live oak—and a conifer, the slash pine (figs. 12 to 15)

Figure 12—The common crapemyrtle represents small trees in this guide.

Figure 13—The southern magnolia represents medium trees in this guide.

Aren Dotterwhy

Figure 14—The live oak represents large trees in this guide.

Aren Dotterwhy

Figure 15—The slash pine represents conifers in this guide.

(see "Common and Scientific Names" section). The selection of these species is based on data availability and representative growth and is not necessarily intended to endorse their use in large numbers.

Tree care costs based on survey findings

Tree dimensions are derived from growth curves developed from street trees in Orlando, Florida (Peper et al. 2009b) (fig. 16). Frequency and costs of tree management are estimated based on data from municipal foresters in Brooksville, Dunedin, Lakeland, Orlando, and St. Petersburg, Florida. In addition, commercial arborists from Ward Reasoner and Sons Landscaping, Inc., Central Florida Tree Services, and Earth Advisors, Inc. provided information on tree management costs on residential properties.

Tree benefits based on numerical models

Benefits are calculated with numerical models and data both from the region (e.g., pollutant emission factors for avoided emissions from energy savings) and from local sources (e.g., Orlando climate data for energy effects). Changes in building energy use from tree shade were based on computer simulations that incorporated building, climate, and shading effects. Sequestration, the net rate of carbon dioxide (CO_2) storage in above- and belowground biomass over the course of one growing season, was calculated using tree growth data and biomass equations for urban trees. Emission reductions were calculated as the product of energy savings and CO_2 emission factors for electricity and heating. Annual consumption of gasoline and diesel fuel by the community forestry divisions was converted into CO_2 equivalent emissions to estimate CO_2 released due to tree maintenance activities. Hourly meteorological data for windspeed, solar radiation and precipitation, as well as hourly concentrations for nitrogen dioxide (NO_2), ozone (O_3), sulfur dioxide (SO_2), and particulate matter (PM_{10}) were used with a numerical model to calculate pollutant dry deposition per tree. Energy savings resulting in reduced emissions of criteria air pollutants (volatile organic compounds [VOCs], NO_2, PM_{10}) from powerplants and space heating equipment were calculated using utility-specific emission factors for electricity and heating fuels. A numerical interception model accounted for the volume of rainfall stored in tree crowns using information on crown projection areas (area under tree **dripline**), leaf areas, and water depths on canopy surfaces with hourly meteorological and rainfall data. The value of aesthetic and other benefits was captured from research that has quantified differences in sales prices of properties that are associated with trees. Anderson and Cordell (1988) found that each large front-yard tree was associated with a 0.88 percent increase in sales price. In this analysis, aesthetic benefits reflect the contribution of a large front-yard tree to local residential sales prices, with adjustments that account for the location of the tree (e.g., front or back yard, residential or commercial land use) and its growth rate.

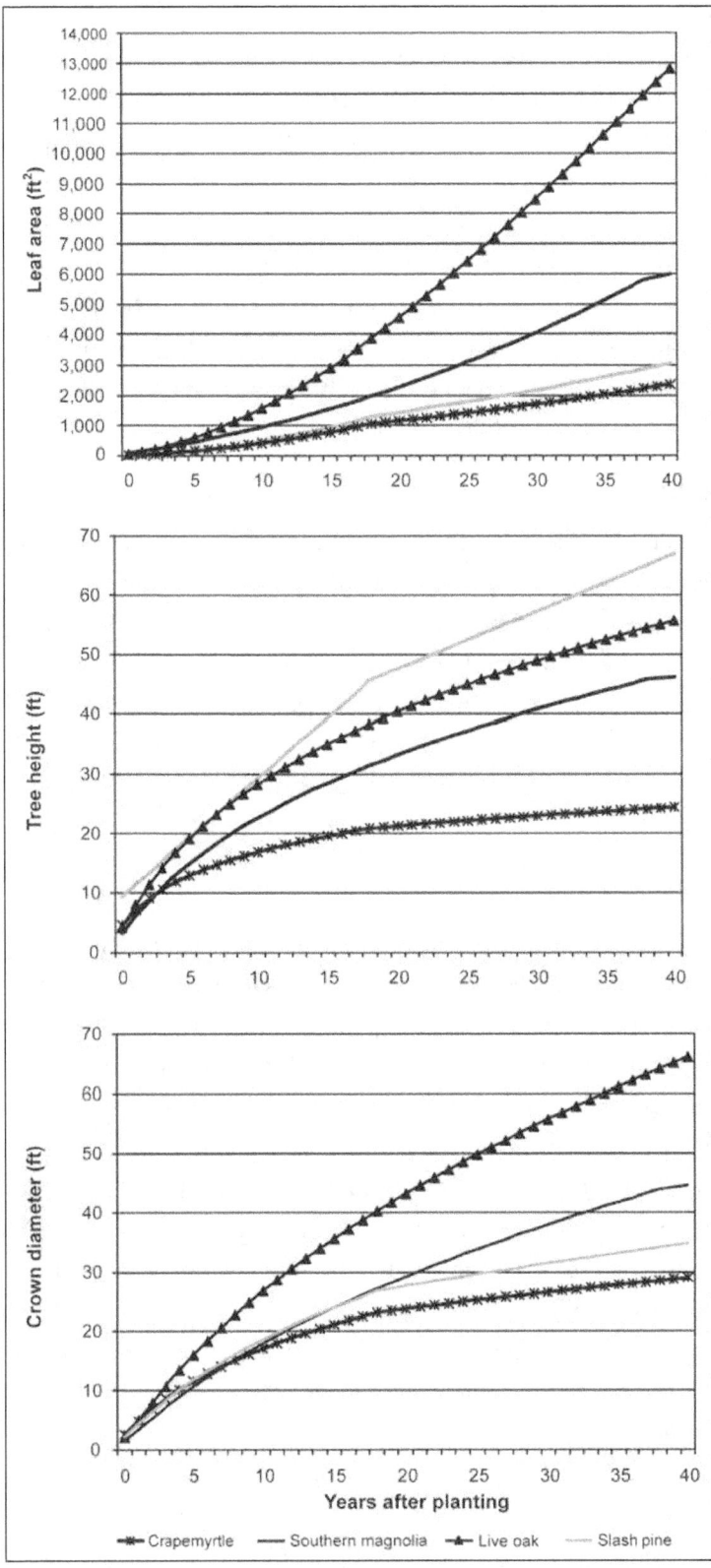

Figure 16—Tree growth curves are based on data collected from street trees in Orlando, Florida. Data for representative small, medium, and large trees are for the common crapemyrtle, southern magnolia, live oak, and slash pine, respectively. Differences in leaf surface area among species are most important for this analysis because functional benefits such as summer shade, rainfall interception, and pollutant uptake are related to leaf surface area.

Regional electricity and natural gas prices are used in this study to quantify the dollar value of energy savings. Costs of preventing or repairing damage from pollution, flooding, or other environmental risks were used to estimate society's **willingness to pay** for clean air and water (Wang and Santini 1995). For example, the value of stormwater runoff reduction owing to rainfall interception by trees is estimated by using marginal **control costs**. If a community or developer is willing to pay an average of $0.01 per gal of treated and controlled runoff to meet minimum standards, then the stormwater runoff mitigation value of a tree that intercepts 1,000 gal of rainfall, eliminating the need for control, should be $10. Appendix 3 contains more detailed information on methods used to calculate benefits and costs and assign monetary value to tree services.

Reporting Results

Tree mortality included

Results are reported in terms of annual value for an average tree. To make these calculations realistic, however, mortality rates are included. Based on our survey of regional municipal foresters and commercial arborists, this analysis assumes that 40 percent of the planted trees will die over the 40-year period, for an annual mortality rate of 1.0 percent per year. This accounting approach "grows" trees in different locations and uses computer simulation to calculate the annual flow of benefits and costs as trees mature and die (McPherson 1992). In appendix 2, results are reported at 5-year intervals for 40 years.

A Note on Palms

Palms in Central Florida

There has been controversy in recent years about the magnitude of the environmental and other benefits of palm trees. Some argue that they have little value and should be avoided in favor of shade trees. Others point to their aesthetic value. Palm trees, especially large-crowned palms, provide shade for cooling, sequester carbon, remove air pollutants from the air, and trap stormwater. At the same time, they can be very expensive to plant and maintain. In Central Florida, our research determined that annual benefits and expenditures for a typical palm used as a street tree (sabal palm) were $4 and $30, respectively, resulting in a net annual loss of $26 per tree. In a municipal forest resource analysis for Orlando, the average annual benefits for sabal palm, Washington fan palm, and queen palm were $5, $8, and $12, respectively. However, management costs specific to palms were not reported (Peper et al. 2009b). The palmetto and fan palm produced fewer benefits than the typical small tree—crapemyrtle.

Many people plant palms believing that they are low maintenance plants, but according to palm expert Dr. Timothy Broschat, they are high maintenance (2010b). He noted that although small, inexpensive container-grown palms are often planted by homeowners, public, commercial, and new development landscapes invariably install larger, field-grown, specimen palms that cost much more to plant. Although structural pruning is not required for palms, non-self-cleaning palms (all of the species grown regularly in the Central Florida region are non-self-cleaning) require that every leaf ever produced by the palm be manually removed from the palm and from the landscape. Fallen fronds do not biodegrade into turf and soil as do the leaves of many broadleaf tree species.

In addition, palms have the highest nutritional requirements of any plant grown in the state. They require routine fertilization with expensive palm fertilizers to maintain full, deficiency symptom-free canopies (Broschat 2010a). The small canopies of most palms are largely owing to nutrient deficiencies such as potassium, which causes premature leaf senescence and discoloration of the older leaves. The discolored older leaves are unsightly and are often removed unnecessarily by tree trimmers. Most palms in Florida landscapes are over-trimmed, to the detriment of the palm's health and functionality (see examples of properly and over-pruned palms at Assessing Damage and Restoring Trees After a Hurricane link in appendix 1). Although the environmental benefits of many small-crowned palms may not exceed the costs of purchasing, installing, and maintaining them, properly maintained palms will live longer, create a better aesthetic "sense of place," and produce more benefits for Florida communities. For more information on palm care, see appendix 1.

Findings of This Study
Average Annual Net Benefits

Average annual net benefits (benefits minus costs) per tree over a 40-year period increase with **mature tree size** (for detailed results see app. 2):

- $1 to $10 for a small tree
- $32 to $51 for a medium tree
- $96 to $123 for a large tree
- $7 to $9 for a conifer

Average annual net benefits increase with tree size

Benefits associated with reduced levels of stormwater runoff and increased property values account for the largest proportion of total benefits in this region. Energy savings, reduced levels of air pollutants and CO_2 in the air are the next most important benefits.

Energy conservation benefits differ with tree location as well as size. Trees located opposite west-facing walls provide the greatest net cooling energy savings. Reducing energy needs reduces CO_2 emissions and thereby reduces atmospheric

CO_2. Similarly, energy savings that reduce demand from powerplants account for important reductions in gases that produce ozone, a major component of smog.

Large broadleaf trees provide the most benefits

Our findings demonstrate that average annual net benefits from large trees like live oak are substantially greater than those from small trees like the crapemyrtle, where public tree maintenance costs exceed benefits returned. Average annual net benefits for the small, medium, and large broadleaf public trees are $1, $32, and $96, respectively. The slash pine, although a large conifer, has a relatively small amount of leaf area; hence, benefits are only slightly greater than the small broadleaf tree values. The largest average annual net benefits from yard trees stemmed from a tree opposite the west-facing wall of a house: $10, $51, $123, and $9 for small, medium, large broadleaf evergreen, and the conifer, respectively.

Net annual benefits at year 40

The large yard tree opposite a west wall produces a net annual benefit of $192 at year 40. In the same location, 40 years after planting, the small, medium, and pine produce annual net benefits of $20, $74, and $27, respectively.

Forty years after planting at a typical public site, the small, medium, and large trees and the conifer provide annual net benefits of $5, $38, $153, and $21, respectively.

Net benefits for a yard tree opposite a west house wall and a public tree also increase with size when summed over the entire 40-year period:

- $403 (yard) and $23 (public) for a small tree
- $2,039 (yard) and $1,266 (public) for a medium tree
- $4,939 (yard) and $3,859 (public) for a large tree
- $344 (yard) and $296 (public) for a conifer

Year 20: environmental benefits exceed tree care costs

Twenty years after planting, average annual benefits for all public trees exceed costs of tree planting and management (tables 1 and 2). For a large live oak in a yard 20 years after planting, the total value of environmental benefits alone ($80) is five times the total annual cost ($16). Environmental benefits total $21, $43, and $16 for the small, medium, and pine tree, whereas tree care costs are lower, $9, $12, and $15, respectively. Adding the value of aesthetics and other benefits to the environmental benefits results in substantial net benefits.

Net benefits are lower for public trees (table 2) than yard trees. Based on our survey findings, public trees are about twice as expensive to maintain as private trees. The standard of care is often high for public trees because of their prominence and potential risk. Also, energy benefits are lower for public trees than for yard trees because public trees are assumed to provide general climate effects, but not to shade buildings directly.

Table 1—Estimated annual benefits and costs for a private tree (residential yard) opposite the west-facing wall 20 years after planting

Benefit category	Common crapemyrtle Small tree 21 ft tall 24-ft spread LSA = 1,211 ft²		Southern magnolia Medium tree 33 ft tall 29-ft spread LSA = 2,346 ft²		Live oak Large tree 40 ft tall 42-ft spread LSA = 4,482 ft²		Slash pine Conifer tree 48 ft tall 28-ft spread LSA = 1,492 ft²	
	Resource units	Total value	Resource units	Total value	Resource units	Total value	Resource units	Total value
		Dollars		*Dollars*		*Dollars*		*Dollars*
Electricity savings ($0.1318/kWh)	100 kWh	13.20	186 kWh	24.49	339 kWh	44.67	37 kWh	4.89
Natural gas savings ($0.0027/kBtu)	5 kBtu	0.01	-6 kBtu	-0.01	-1 kBtu	0.00	46 kBtu	0.12
Carbon dioxide ($0.003/lb)	266 lb	0.89	468 lb	1.56	1,006 lb	3.36	195 lb	0.65
Ozone ($2.20/lb)	0.40 lb	0.88	0.79 lb	1.74	1.65 lb	3.63	0.70 lb	1.54
Nitrous oxide ($2.20/lb)	0.21 lb	0.47	0.42 lb	0.91	0.81 lb	1.79	0.16 lb	0.36
Sulfur dioxide ($2.01/lb)	0.15 lb	0.30	0.29 lb	0.59	0.57 lb	1.14	0.09 lb	0.18
Small particulate matter ($2.10/lb)	0.17 lb	0.36	0.36 lb	0.76	0.65 lb	1.37	0.25 lb	0.53
Volatile organic compounds ($1.03/lb)	0.06 lb	0.07	0.12 lb	0.13	0.24 lb	0.25	0.04 lb	0.04
Biogenic volatile organic compounds ($1.03/lb)	0 lb	0.00	-1.21 lb	-1.25	-2.75 lb	-2.84	-0.03 lb	-0.03
Rainfall interception ($0.003/gal)	1,749 gal	5.25	4,657 gal	13.97	8,854 gal	26.56	2,711 gal	8.13
Environmental subtotal		21.43		42.88		79.92		16.41
Other benefits		9.95		30.66		69.98		13.07
Total benefits		31.38		73.55		149.90		29.48
Total costs		9.30		11.61		16.18		14.73
Net benefits		22.08		61.94		133.72		14.76

LSA = leaf surface area.

33

Table 2—Estimated annual benefits and costs for a public tree (street/park) 20 years after planting

Benefit category	Common crapemyrtle Small tree 21 ft tall 24-ft spread LSA = 1,211 ft²		Southern magnolia Medium tree 33 ft tall 29-ft spread LSA = 2,346 ft²		Live oak Large tree 40 ft tall 42-ft spread LSA = 4,482 ft²		Slash pine Conifer tree 48 ft tall 28-ft spread LSA = 1,492 ft²	
	Resource units	Total value	Resource units	Total value	Resource units	Total value	Resource units	Total value
		Dollars		Dollars		Dollars		Dollars
Electricity savings ($0.0788/kWh)	27 kWh	3.50	42 kWh	5.53	91 kWh	11.95	37 kWh	4.89
Natural gas savings ($0.0110/kBtu)	14 kBtu	0.04	21 kBtu	0.06	42 kBtu	0.11	46 kBtu	0.12
Carbon dioxide ($0.003/lb)	118 lb	0.39	178 lb	0.59	505 lb	1.69	195 lb	0.65
Ozone ($0.61/lb)	0.40 lb	0.88	0.79 lb	1.74	1.65 lb	3.63	0.70 lb	1.54
Nitrous oxide ($0.61/lb)	0.21 lb	0.47	0.42 lb	0.91	0.81 lb	1.79	0.16 lb	0.36
Sulfur dioxide ($1.42/lb)	0.15 lb	0.30	0.29 lb	0.59	0.57 lb	1.14	0.09 lb	0.18
Small particulate matter ($1.14/lb)	0.17 lb	0.36	0.36 lb	0.76	0.65 lb	1.37	0.25 lb	0.53
Volatile organic compounds ($0.19/lb)	0.06 lb	0.07	0.12 lb	0.13	0.24 lb	0.25	0.04 lb	0.04
Biogenic volatile organic compounds ($0.19/lb)	0 lb	0.00	-1.21 lb	-1.25	-2.75 lb	-2.84	0 lb	-0.03
Rainfall interception ($0.003/gal)	1,749 gal	5.25	4,657 gal	13.97	8,854 gal	26.56	2,711 gal	8.13
Environmental subtotal		11.26		23.03		45.64		16.41
Other benefits		11.28		34.75		79.30		14.81
Total benefits		22.54		57.77		124.94		31.22
Total costs		19.30		22.20		28.82		25.29
Net benefits		3.24		35.57		96.12		5.93

LSA = leaf surface area.

Average Annual Costs

Averaged over 40 years, the costs for yard and public trees, respectively, are as follows:

- $20 and $22 for a small tree
- $23 and $27 for a medium tree
- $25 and $31 for a large tree
- $23 and $27 for a conifer

Costs increase with mature tree size because of added expenses for pruning and removing larger trees.

Over the 40-year period, tree planting is the single greatest cost for yard trees, averaging $11 per tree per year (see app. 2, table 7). Based on our survey, we assume in this study that a 3-in **caliper** (16-ft overall height) yard tree is planted at a cost of $440; the price includes the tree, labor, and any necessary watering during the establishment period. For public trees, pruning ($7 to $11 per tree per year) and tree planting ($6 per tree per year) are the greatest costs. Annual removal and disposal costs are significant for yard trees, ranging from $6 to $10 over the four tree types. Pruning, annualized over 40 years, averages $1 to $3 per tree. At $4 to $6 per tree per year, removal and disposal costs are also significant for public trees, as are administrative costs ($3 to $4 per tree) in this hurricane-prone region.

Table 3 shows annual management costs 20 years after planting for yard trees to the west of a house and for public trees. Annual costs for yard trees range from $9 to $16, and public tree care costs are $19 to $29. In general, public trees are more expensive to maintain than yard trees because of their prominence, the greater need for public safety, and conflicts with infrastructure.

Average Annual Benefits

Average annual benefits over 40 years, including energy savings, stormwater runoff reduction, aesthetic value, air quality improvement, and CO_2 sequestration increase with mature tree size (figs. 17 and 18; for detailed results see app. 2):

- $23 to $30 for a small tree
- $59 to $74 for a medium tree
- $127 to $149 for a large tree
- $32 to $34 for a conifer

Stormwater runoff reduction—
Stormwater runoff reduction services by trees that intercept rain before it reaches a stormwater treatment system are the most significant environmental benefit provided by trees. The live oak intercepts 12,141 gal per year on average over a 40-year

35

Table 3—Estimated annual costs 20 years after planting for a private tree opposite the west-facing wall and a public tree

Costs	Common crapemyrtle Small tree 21 ft tall 24-ft spread LSA = 1,211 ft²		Southern magnolia Medium tree 33 ft tall 29-ft spread LSA = 2,346 ft²		Live oak Large tree 40 ft tall 42-ft spread LSA = 4,482 ft²		Slash pine Conifer tree 48 ft tall 28-ft spread LSA = 1,492 ft²	
	Private: west	Public tree	Private: west	Public tree	Private: west	Public tree	Private: west	Public tree
	Dollars per tree per year							
Pruning	1.09	9.00	1.09	9.00	4.37	14.00	4.37	14.00
Remove and dispose	6.47	4.28	8.29	5.48	9.31	6.16	8.17	5.40
Pest and disease	0.20	0.22	0.26	0.29	0.29	0.32	0.26	0.28
Infrastructure	0.19	1.68	0.24	2.15	0.27	2.41	0.24	2.12
Irrigation	0.00	0.00	0.00	0.00	0.00	0.00	0.00	0.00
Cleanup	0.09	0.79	0.12	1.01	0.13	1.14	0.11	1.00
Liability and legal	0.02	0.18	0.03	0.23	0.03	0.26	0.03	0.23
Administration and other	1.23	3.15	1.57	4.03	1.77	4.53	1.55	2.27
Total costs	9.30	19.30	11.61	22.20	16.18	28.82	14.73	25.29
Total benefits	31.38	22.54	73.55	57.77	149.90	124.94	29.48	31.22
Total net benefits	22.08	3.24	61.94	35.57	133.72	96.12	14.76	5.93

Note: Prices for removal and disposal are included to account for expected mortality of citywide planting.
LSA = leaf surface area.

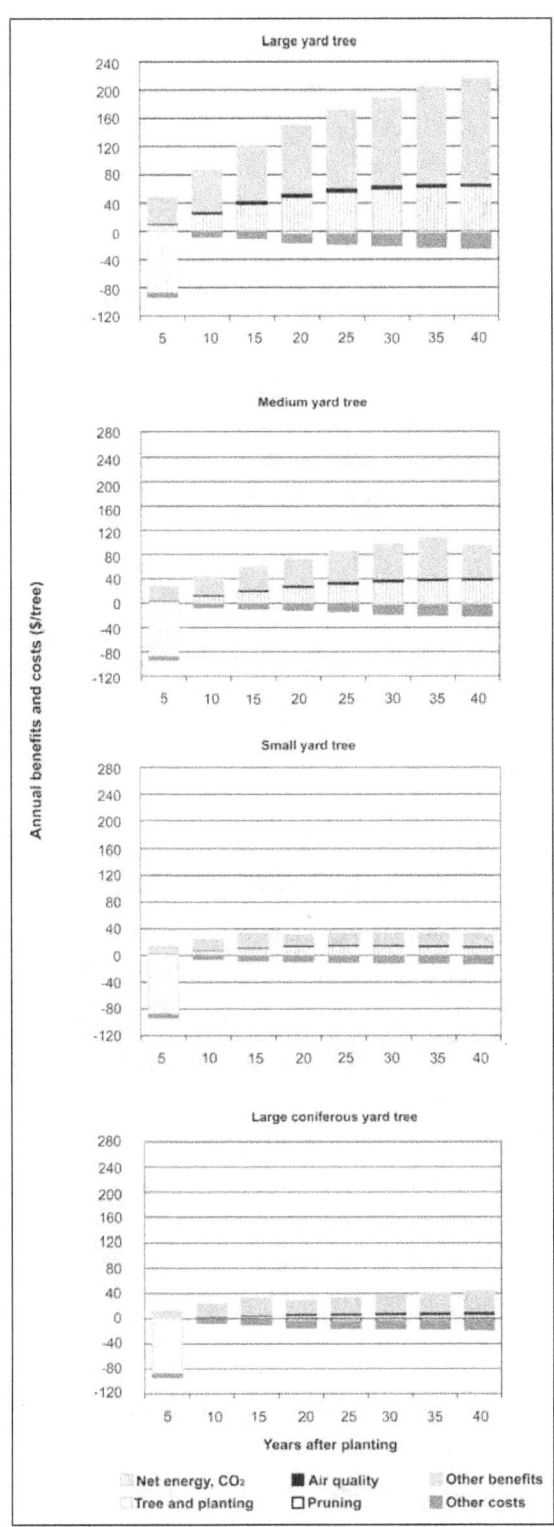

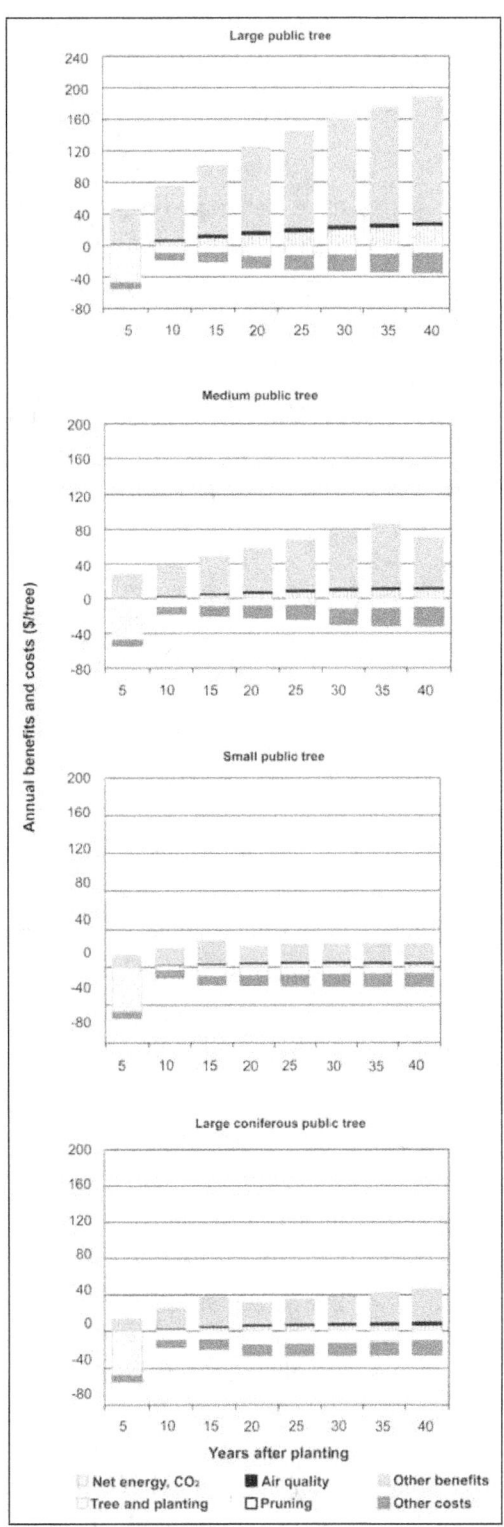

Figure 17—Estimated annual benefits and costs for a small (common crapemyrtle), medium (southern magnolia), large (live oak), and a conifer (slash pine) tree located west of a residence. Costs are greatest during the initial establishment period, whereas benefits increase with tree size.

Figure 18—Estimated annual benefits and costs for public small (common crapemyrtle), medium (southern magnolia), large (live oak), and a conifer (slash pine) tree.

period with an implied value of $36 (app. 2, table 12). The crapemyrtle, southern magnolia, and slash pine intercept 1,573, 6,191, and 3,084 gal per year on average, with values of $5, 19, and $9, respectively (app. 2, tables 6, 9, and 15). Forty years after planting, average stormwater runoff reductions equal 2,251, 13,124, 27,449, and 6,317 gal, respectively, for the small, medium, large, and conifer trees. The hydrology modeling was based on 2008 rainfall data for the Orlando International Airport (53 in per year); other, wetter parts of the Central Florida region can expect much higher benefits.

Stormwater benefits are crucial

As the cities of the Central Florida region continue to grow, the amount of impervious surface will continue to increase. The role that trees, in combination with other strategies such as rain gardens and structural soils, can play in reducing stormwater runoff is substantial.

Energy savings—

Energy benefits are the second most significant environmental benefit and tend to increase with mature tree size. For example, average annual energy benefits over the 40-year period are $11 for the small crapemyrtle tree opposite a west-facing wall and $42 for the larger live oak. For species of all sizes, energy savings increase as trees mature and their leaf surface area increases (figs. 17 and 18).

As expected in a region with warm summers and mild winters, cooling savings account for most of the total energy benefit. Trees planted on the west side of buildings have the greatest energy benefits because the effect of shade on cooling costs is maximized by blocking the sun during the warmest time of the day. A yard tree located south of a home produced the least total benefit because, at the lower latitudes of the Central Florida region where the sun remains mostly overhead throughout the year, less sunlight strikes a building on the south side. Trees located east of a building provided intermediate benefits. Total energy benefits also reflect species-related traits such as size, form, branch pattern, and density, as well as time in leaf.

Average annual total energy benefits for public trees were less than for yard trees and ranged from $3 for the crapemyrtle to $13 for the large live oak.

Air quality improvement—

Air quality benefits are defined as the sum of pollutant uptake by trees and avoided powerplant emissions from energy savings minus biogenic volatile organic compounds (BVOCs) released by trees. Average annual air quality benefits over the 40-year period were approximately $2 to $4 per tree. These relatively low air quality benefits reflect the clean air of most cities in the Central Florida region. Contrast these results with the air quality benefits of a large tree in the Northeast ($13; McPherson et al. 2007), Midwest ($8; McPherson et al. 2006c), and southern California ($28; McPherson et al. 2000).

The ability of trees to intercept O_3 from the air is the most highly valued. The large-stature live oak produces the greatest benefit because of its size. Over 40 years it is estimated to reduce an average of 1.99 lb of O_3 from the air annually, valued at $4.37. Average annual reductions in NO_2, SO_2, PM_{10}, and volatile organic compounds (VOCs) for the large tree are valued at $1.78, $1.10, $1.77, and $0.24, respectively. This oak is a high emitter of BVOCs; however, the large amount of leaf area associated with these populations result in substantial net air quality benefits.

Forty years after planting, the average annual monetary values of air quality improvement (avoided + uptake of pollutants) for the crapemyrtle, southern magnolia, live oak, and slash pine are $1.90, $2.59, 4.22, and $2.61, respectively.

Carbon dioxide reduction—

Net atmospheric CO_2 reductions accrue for all tree types. Average annual net reductions range from a high of 1,025 lb ($3.42) for a large live oak on the west side of a house to a low of 99 lbs ($0.33) for a small public crapemyrtle. Deciduous trees opposite west-facing house walls generally produce the greatest CO_2 reduction from reduced powerplant emissions associated with energy savings. The values for the crapemyrtle are lowest for CO_2 reduction because of the relatively small impacts of shade from the small-growing tree on energy consumption and emission reductions.

Forty years after planting, average annual avoided emissions and sequestered and released CO_2 for a yard tree opposite a west wall are 220, 462, 1,025, and 151 lb, respectively, for the small, medium, and large broadleaf trees and the conifer.

Aesthetic and other benefits—

Benefits associated with property value account for the largest portion of total benefits. As trees grow and become more visible, they can increase a property's sales price. Average annual values associated with these aesthetic and other benefits for yard trees are $12, $28, $63, and $15, for the small, medium, and large broadleaf evergreen trees and for the conifer, respectively. The values for public trees are $13, $31, $72, and $17, respectively. The values for yard trees are slightly less than for public trees because offstreet trees contribute less to a property's curb appeal than more prominent street trees. Because these estimates are based on median home sale prices, the effects of trees on property values and aesthetics will vary depending on local economies and market fluctuations.

Aesthetic benefits are substantial

Chapter 4. Estimating Benefits and Costs for Tree Planting Projects in Your Community

Using hypothetical examples, this chapter shows two ways that benefit-cost information presented in this guide can be used. The first example demonstrates how to adjust values from the guide for local conditions when the goal is to estimate benefits and costs for a proposed tree planting project. The second example explains how to compare net benefits derived from planting different types of trees. The Center for Urban Forest Research has developed a computer program called i-Tree Streets (formerly STRATUM), part of the i-Tree software suite, that simplifies these calculations for analysis of existing street tree populations (http://www. itreetools.org) in a complete or sample inventory and will produce a "snapshot" of the structure, function, and value of trees. The program produces detailed reports, including benefit and cost estimates, for a single year. The methods detailed in the following examples allow users to estimate benefits and costs using a typical small, medium, and large broadleaf tree, and a conifer for a 40-year period. As mentioned previously, the goal is to provide a general accounting of the value of services provided by the trees, as well as the costs they incur. The last section discusses actions communities can take to increase the cost-effectiveness of their tree programs.

Applying Benefit-Cost Data

Hurston Park Example

The hypothetical city of Hurston Park is located in the Central Florida region and has a population of 74,000. Most of its street trees were planted decades ago, with laurel oak and crapemyrtle (see "Common and Scientific Names" section) as the dominant species. Currently, the tree canopy cover is sparse because a recent hurricane and a pest destroyed many of the laurel oaks and they have not been replaced. Many of the remaining street trees are in declining health. The city hired an urban forester 2 years ago and an active citizens' group, the Green Team, has formed (fig. 19).

Initial discussions among the Green Team, local utilities, the urban forester, and other partners led to a proposed urban forestry program. The program intends to plant 1,000 trees in Hurston Park over a 5-year period. Trained volunteers will plant 2-in-caliper trees in the following proportions: 70 percent large-maturing trees, 15 percent medium-maturing trees, 5 percent small-maturing trees, and 10 percent conifers. One hundred trees will be planted in parks, and the remaining 900 trees will be planted along Main Street and other downtown streets following guidelines for selecting and planting wind-resistant trees. Mortality rates for earlier planting

USDA Forest Service, PSW, Center for Urban Forest Research

Figure 19—The (hypothetical) Green Team is motivated to re-green their community by planting 1,000 trees in 5 years.

projects have been high, so the Green Team and the urban forester will concentrate their planting efforts in areas that are likely to be most successful, including planting spaces with sufficient soil capacity for trees to grow and as little conflict with infrastructure as possible, and that maximize environmental benefits. They expect to find a number of good suggestions for planting in chapter 5 of this guide and from the University of Florida/Institute of Food and Agriculture Sciences Extension Web sites (UF/IFAS) for urban forestry (see app. 1).

The Hurston Park City Council has agreed to maintain the current funding level for management of existing trees. Also, they will advocate formation of a municipal tree district to raise funds for the proposed tree-planting project. A municipal tree district is similar in concept to a landscape assessment district, which receives revenues based on formulas that account for the services different customers receive. For example, the proximity of customers to greenspace in a landscape assessment district may determine how much they pay for upkeep. A municipal tree district might receive funding from air quality districts, stormwater management agencies, electric utilities, businesses, and residents in proportion to the value of future benefits these groups will receive from trees in terms of air quality, hydrology, energy, carbon dioxide (CO_2), and property value. The formation of such a district would require voter approval of a special assessment that charges recipients for tree planting and maintenance costs in proportion to the benefits they receive from the new trees. The council needs to know the amount of funding required for tree planting and maintenance, as well as how the benefits will be distributed over the 40-year life of the project.

As a first step, the Hurston Park city forester and Green Team decided to use the values in appendix 2, tables 6 to 17, to quantify total cumulative benefits and costs over 40 years for the proposed planting of 1,000 public trees—700 large, 150 medium, and 50 small broadleaf evergreen along with 100 pines.

Before setting up a spreadsheet to calculate benefits and costs, the team considered which aspects of Hurston Park's urban and community forestry project differ from the regional values used in this guide (the methods for calculating the values in appendix 2 are described in appendix 3):

1. The price of electricity in Hurston Park is $0.1143 per kWh, not $0.132 per kWh as used in this guide. It is assumed that the buildings that will be shaded by the new street trees have air conditioning.

2. The community recently voted to increase funding for improved flood control to protect surrounding wetlands, increasing the price of stormwater treatment from $0.003 per gallon used in this guide to $0.004 per gallon.

3. The Green Team projected future annual costs for monitoring tree health and implementing their stewardship program. Administration costs are estimated to average $1,500 annually for the life of the trees or $1.50 per tree each year. This guide assumed an average annual administration cost of about $2.00 per tree. Thus, an adjustment is necessary.

4. Planting will cost $225 per tree. The guide assumes planting costs of $230 per tree. The costs will be lower for Hurston Park because purchase price is slightly lower from a local grower.

To calculate the dollar value of total benefits and costs for the 40-year period, the forester created a spreadsheet table (table 4). Each benefit and cost category is listed in the first column. Prices, adjusted where necessary for Hurston Park, are entered into the second column. The third column contains the **resource units** (RUs) per tree per year associated with the benefit or the cost per tree per year,

The first step: determine tree planting numbers

Table 4—Spreadsheet calculations of benefits and costs for the Hurston Park planting project (1,000 trees) over 40 years

Benefits	Price (adjusted)	700 large trees		150 medium trees		50 small trees		100 conifer trees		1,000 total trees		Percentage of positive services
		Annual per tree	Total value	Annual per tree	Total value	Annual per tree	Total value	Annual per tree	Total value	Total value	Annual per tree	Percent
	Dollars	Resource units	Dollars	Resource units	Dollars	Resource units	Dollars	Resource units	Dollars	Dollars	Dollars	Percent
Electricity (kWh)	0.1143	97.11	310,791	43.61	29,908	21.82	4,988	32.46	14,841	360,527	9.01	8.14
Natural gas (kBtu)	0.0027	41	3,075	21	337	12	64	40	429	3,905	0.10	0.09
Net carbon dioxide (lb)	0.0033	584	54,616	187	3,747	99	661	151	2,017	61,042	1.53	1.38
Ozone (lb)	2.20	1.99	122,393	0.92	12,125	0.39	1,713	0.68	5,975	142,206	3.56	3.21
Nitrous oxide (lb)	2.20	0.81	49,818	0.42	5,535	0.18	791	0.15	1,318	57,462	1.44	1.30
Sulfur dioxide (lb)	2.01	0.55	30,892	0.29	3,490	0.12	481	0.08	642	35,505	0.89	0.80
Small particulate matter (lb)	2.10	0.84	49,408	0.46	5,798	0.17	714	0.31	2,605	58,525	1.46	1.32
Volatile organic compounds (lb)	1.03	0.23	6,655	0.12	744	0.05	103	0.03	124	7,627	0.19	0.17
Biogenic volatile organic compounds (lb)	1.03	-4.88	-141,207	-1.98	-12,277	0.00	0	-0.06	-248	-153,733	-3.84	-3.47
Hydrology (gal)	0.0040	12,141	1,359,792	6,191	148,584	1,573	12,584	3,084	49,344	1,570,304	39.26	35.46
Aesthetics and other benefits ($)		71.50	2,002,000	31.43	188,580	13.10	26,200	16.95	67,800	2,284,580	57.11	51.59
Total benefits			3,848,231		386,572		48,301		144,846	4,427,950	110.70	100.00

Costs	Price (adjusted)	Annual per tree	Total value	Annual per tree	Total value	Annual per tree	Total value	Annual per tree	Total value	Total value	Annual per tree	Percentage of costs
	Dollars	‑‑‑‑‑‑‑‑‑‑‑‑‑‑‑‑‑‑‑‑‑‑‑‑‑‑‑‑‑‑‑ Dollars ‑‑‑‑‑‑‑‑‑‑‑‑‑‑‑‑‑‑‑‑‑‑‑‑‑‑‑‑‑‑‑										Percent
Tree and planting	225	5.63	157,500	5.63	33,750	5.63	11,250	5.63	22,500	225,000	5.63	20.80
Pruning		10.12	283,334	8.54	51,268	6.83	13,654	10.63	42,539	390,795	9.77	36.13
Remove and dispose		6.27	175,697	5.60	33,589	4.13	8,264	4.92	19,675	237,225	5.93	21.93
Pest and disease		0.30	8,504	0.27	1,621	0.20	406	0.24	964	11,495	0.29	1.06
Infrastructure repair		2.26	63,408	2.01	12,087	1.51	3,027	1.80	7,187	85,708	2.14	7.9
Irrigation		0.24	6,790	0.24	1,455	0.24	485	0.24	960	9,690	0.24	0.92
Cleanup		1.07	29,935	0.95	5,706	0.71	1,429	0.85	3,393	40,463	1.01	3.74
Liability and legal		0.24	6,803	0.22	1,297	0.16	325	0.19	771	9,196	0.23	0.85
Admin and other	1.50	1.50	42,000	2.50	15,000	2.50	5,000	2.50	10,000	72,000	1.80	6.66
Total costs			773,972		155,773		43,839		107,988	1,081,572	27.04	100.00
Net benefit			3,074,260		230,799		4,461		36,858	3,346,378	83.66	
Benefit/cost ratio			4.97		2.48		1.10		1.34	4.09		
(Net benefit per tree)			109.79		38.47		2.23		9.21	83.66		

Note: Adjusted values are for electricity, natural gas, tree and planting, and admin and other costs.

which can be found in appendix 2. For aesthetic and other benefits, the dollar values for public trees are placed in the RU columns. The fourth column lists the 40-year total values, obtained by multiplying the RU values by tree numbers, prices, and 40 years.

To adjust for lower electricity prices, the forester multiplied electricity saved for a large public tree in the RU column (97.11 kWh) by the Hurston Park price for electricity ($0.1143/kWh) by the number of trees planted and 40 years (97.11 x $0.1143 x 700 x 40 = $310,791) to obtain cumulative air-conditioning energy savings for the large public trees (table 4). The process was carried out for all benefits and all tree types.

Similarly, to adjust for higher cost of stormwater retention and treatment, the forester multiplied stormwater intercepted by a large public tree in the RU column (12,141 gal) by the new price for retaining and treating the water ($0.004 per gallon) and the number of trees over the 40-year period for a cumulative value of $1,359,792.

To adjust cost figures, the city forester changed the planting cost from $230 assumed in the guide to $225 (table 4). This planting cost was annualized by dividing the cost per tree by 40 years ($225 ÷ 40 = $5.63 per tree per year). Total planting costs were calculated by multiplying this value by 700 large trees and 40 years ($157,500).

The administration, inspection, and outreach costs are expected to average $1.50 per tree per year. Consequently, the total administration cost for large trees is $1.50 × 700 large trees × 40 years ($42,000). The same procedure was followed to calculate costs for the medium and small trees.

All costs and all benefits were summed. Subtracting total costs from total benefits yields net benefits over the 40-year period:

- $3.1 million for 700 large trees
- $230,799 for 150 medium trees
- $4,461 for 50 small trees
- $36,858 for 100 conifers

Annual benefits over 40 years total $4.4 million ($111 per tree per year), and annual costs total about $1.1 million ($27 per tree per year). The total annual net benefits for all 1,000 trees over the 40-year period are $3.3 million. To calculate this average annual net benefit per tree, the forester divided the total net benefit by the number of trees planted (1,000) and 40 years ($3,346,378 ÷ 1,000 trees ÷ 40 years = $83.66). Dividing total benefits by total costs yielded benefit-cost ratios (BCRs) of 1.10, 2.48, 4.97, and 1.34 for small, medium, and large broadleaf trees and conifers,

The second step: adjust for local prices of benefits

The third step: adjust for local costs

The fourth step: calculate net benefits and benefit-cost ratios for public trees

respectively. The BCR for the entire planting is 4.09, indicating that $4.09 will be returned for every $1 invested.

It is important to remember that this analysis assumes 40 percent of the planted trees die and are not replaced. Also, it does not account for the time value of money from a capital investment perspective. Use the municipal discount rate to compare this investment in tree planting and management with alternative municipal investments.

The final step: determine how services are distributed, and link these to sources of revenue

The city forester and Green Team now know that the project will cost about $1.1 million, and the average annual cost will be about $27,000 ($1,080,612 ÷ 40 years); however, expenditures are front-loaded because relatively more funds will be needed initially for planting and stewardship. The fifth and last step is to identify the distribution of services that the trees will provide. The last column in table 4 shows the distribution of services as a percentage of the total:

- Stormwater runoff reduction = 35.5 percent
- Energy savings = 8.2 percent (cooling = 8.1 percent, heating = 0.1 percent)
- Air quality improvement = 3.3 percent
- CO_2 reduction = 1.4 percent
- Aesthetics/property value increase = 51.6 percent

With this information, the planning team can determine how to distribute the costs for tree planting and maintenance based on who benefits from the services the trees will provide. For example, assuming the goal is to generate enough annual revenue to cover the total costs of managing the trees ($1.1 million), fees could be distributed in the following manner:

- $383,600 from the stormwater management district for water quality improvement associated with reduced runoff (35.5 percent).
- $88,600 from electric and natural gas utilities for peak energy savings (8.2 percent). (Utility companies invest in planting trees because it is more cost effective to reduce peak energy demand than to meet peak needs through added infrastructure.)
- $35,700, from air quality management district for net reduction in air pollutants (3.3 percent).
- $15,100 from local industry for atmospheric CO_2 reductions (1.4 percent).
- $557,600 from property owners for increased property values (51.6 percent).

Whether funds are sought from partners, the general fund, homeowners associations, or other sources, this information can assist managers in developing policy, setting priorities, and making decisions.

City of Marcusville Example

Ten years ago, as a municipal cost-cutting measure, the hypothetical city of Marcusville stopped planting street trees in areas of new development. Instead, developers were required to plant front yard trees, thereby reducing costs to the city. The community forester and concerned citizens came to notice that instead of the large, stately trees the city had once planted, developers were planting small flowering trees, which were more aesthetically pleasing in early years, but would never achieve the stature—or the benefits—of larger shade trees. To evaluate the consequences of these changes, the community forester and citizens decided to compare the benefits of planting small, medium, and large trees for a hypothetical street-tree planting project in a new neighborhood in Marcusville.

As a first step, the city forester and concerned citizens decided to quantify the total cumulative benefits and costs over 40 years for three potential street tree planting scenarios in Marcusville. The scenarios compare plantings of 500 small trees, 500 medium trees, and 500 large trees. Data in appendix 2 are used for the calculations; however, three aspects of Marcusville's urban and community forestry program are different from those assumed in this tree guide:

The first step: calculate benefits and costs over 40 years

1. The price of electricity is $0.075/kWh, not $0.132/kWh.

2. The city will provide irrigation for the first 5 years at a cost of approximately $0.50 per tree annually.

3. Planting costs are $200 per tree for trees instead of $230 per tree.

To calculate the dollar value of total benefits for the 40-year period, values from the last columns in the benefit tables in appendix 2 (40-year average) are multiplied by 40 years. As this value is for one tree, it must be multiplied by the total number of trees planted in the respective small, medium, or large tree size classes. To adjust for lower electricity prices, we multiply electricity saved for each tree type in the RU column by the number of trees and 40 years (large tree: 97 kWh × 500 trees × 40 years = 1,940,000 kWh). This value is multiplied by the price of electricity in Marcusville ($0.075/kWh × 1,940,000 kWh = $145,600) to obtain cumulative air-conditioning energy savings for the project (table 5).

The second step: adjust for local prices of benefits

All the benefits are summed for each size tree for a 40-year period. The 500 small trees provide $434,600 in total benefits. The medium and large trees provide about $1.1 and $2.4 million, respectively.

To adjust cost figures, we add a value for irrigation by multiplying the annual cost by the number of trees and by the number of years that irrigation will be applied ($0.50 × 500 trees × 5 years = $1,250). We multiply 500 trees by the unit

Table 5—Spreadsheet calculations of benefits and costs for the Marcusville planting project (1,500 trees) over 40 years

Benefits	Price (adjusted)	500 large		500 medium		500 small		1,500 tree total		
		Resource units	Total value	Resource units	Total value	Resource units	Total value	Resource units	Total value	Average /tree
	Dollars		Dollars		Dollars		Dollars		Dollars	Dollars
Electricity (kWh)	0.08	1,940,000	145,600	880,000	66,000	440,000	33,000	3,260,000	244,600	163.07
Natural gas (kBtu)	0.0027	820,000	2,200	420,000	1,200	240,000	600	1,480,000	4,000	2.67
Net carbon dioxide (lb)	0.0033	11,680,000	39,000	3,740,000	12,400	1,980,000	6,600	17,400,000	58,000	38.67
Ozone (lb)	2.20	39,760	87,400	18,480	40,600	7,750	17,000	65,990	145,000	96.67
Nitrous oxide (lb)	2.20	16,230	35,600	8,430	18,600	3,570	7,800	28,230	62,000	41.33
Sulfur dioxide (lb)	2.01	10,990	22,000	5,830	11,600	2,470	5,000	19,290	38,600	25.73
Small particulate matter (lb)	2.10	16,870	35,400	9,160	19,200	3,380	7,200	29,410	61,800	41.20
Volatile organic compounds (lb)	1.03	4,590	4,800	2,450	2,600	1,050	1,000	8,090	8,400	5.60
Biogenic volatile organic compounds (lb)	1.03	-97,590	-100,800	-39,530	-40,800	0	0	-137,120	-141,600	-94.40
Hydrology (gal)	0.0030	242,820,000	728,400	123,820,000	371,400	31,460,000	94,400	398,100,000	1,194,200	796.13
Aesthetics and other benefits ($)			1,430,000		628,600		262,000		2,320,600	1,547.07
Total benefits			2,429,600		1,131,400		434,600		3,995,600	2,663.73

Costs		Total value	Total value	Total value	Total value	
			———————— Dollars ————————		Total value	
Tree and planting	200	100,000	100,000	100,000	300,000	200.00
Pruning		202,381	170,893	136,543	509,816	339.88
Remove and dispose		125,498	111,964	82,636	320,097	213.40
Pest and disease		6,074	5,404	4,060	15,538	10.36
Infrastructure		45,291	40,289	30,269	115,850	77.23
Irrigation	0.06	1,250	1,250	1,250	3,750	2.50
Cleanup		21,382	19,021	14,290	54,693	36.46
Liability and legal		4,860	4,323	3,248	12,430	8.29
Admin and other		85,043	75,651	56,835	217,529	145.02
Total costs		591,780	528,793	429,130	1,549,703	1,033.13
Net benefits		1,837,820	602,607	5,470	2,445,897	1,630.60
Benefit/cost ratio		4.11	2.14	1.01	2.58	
(Net benefit per tree)		3,676	1,205	11	1,631	

Note: Adjusted values are for electricity, tree and planting, and irrigation.

planting cost ($200) to obtain the adjusted cost for planting (500 × $200 = $100,000). The average annual 40-year costs taken from the cost tables in appendix 2 for other items are multiplied by 40 years and the number of trees to compute total costs. These 40-year cost values are entered into table 5.

The third step: adjust for local costs

Subtracting total costs from total benefits yields net benefits for the small ($5,470), medium ($602,607), and large ($1,837,820) trees. The total net benefit for the 40-year period is about $2.4 million or $1,631 per tree ($2,445,897 ÷ 1,500 trees) on average (table 5).

The net benefits per street tree over the 40-year period are as follows:

- $11 for a small tree
- $1,205 for a medium tree
- $3,676 for a large tree

When small trees are planted instead of large trees, the residents of Marcusville stand to lose over $3,600 per tree in benefits foregone. In a new neighborhood with 500 small trees, the total loss of net benefits would exceed $1.8 million over the project lifetime. Planting all small trees would result in net benefits of $16,411 (3 x 5,470). If 1,500 large trees were planted the benefits would exceed $5.5 million. Planting all small trees would cost the city well over $5 million in ecosystem services forgone.

The fourth step: calculate cost savings and benefits foregone

Based on this analysis, the city of Marcusville decided to develop and enforce a street tree ordinance that requires planting large trees where space permits and requires tree shade plans that show how developers will achieve 50 percent shade over streets, sidewalks, and parking lots within 15 years of development.

This analysis assumes that 40 percent of the planted trees died. It does not account for the time value of money from a capital investment perspective, but this could be done by using the municipal discount rate.

Increasing Program Cost-Effectiveness

What if the program you have designed looks promising in terms of stormwater-runoff reduction, energy savings, volunteer participation, and additional benefits, but the costs are too high? This section describes some steps to consider that may increase benefits and reduce costs, thereby increasing cost-effectiveness.

What if costs are too high?

Increasing Benefits

Improved stewardship to increase the health and survival of recently planted trees is one strategy for increasing cost-effectiveness. An evaluation of the Sacramento Shade program found that tree survival rates had a substantial impact on projected

Work to increase survival rates

Customize planting locations

benefits (Hildebrandt et al. 1996). Higher survival rates increase energy savings and reduce tree removal and planting costs.

Energy benefits can be further increased by planting a higher percentage of trees in locations that produce the greatest energy savings, such as opposite west-facing walls and close to buildings with air conditioning. By customizing tree locations to increase numbers in high-yield sites, energy savings can be boosted.

Conifers and broadleaf evergreens intercept rainfall and particulate matter year round as well as provide shade, which lowers cooling costs. Locating these types of trees in yards, parks, school grounds, and other open-space areas can increase benefits.

Reducing Program Costs

Cost effectiveness is influenced by program costs as well as benefits:

Cost effectiveness = Total net benefit ÷ total program cost

Cutting costs is one strategy to increase cost effectiveness. A substantial percentage of total program costs occur during the first 5 years and are associated with tree planting and establishment (McPherson 1993). Some strategies to reduce these costs include:

Reduce up-front and establishment costs

- Plant bare-root or smaller tree stock.
- Use trained volunteers for planting and young tree care, irrigation, and structural pruning (fig.20).
- Provide followup care to increase tree survival and reduce replacement costs.
- Select and locate trees to avoid conflicts with infrastructure.
- Select high-quality nursery stock with well-formed roots and crowns (Florida #1 or Florida Fancy), which often results in reduced pavement damage, improved survival, and less pruning.
- Select wind-resistant species.
- Maintain a single dominant leader by pruning young trees to reduce future pruning costs. Also, prune young trees to eliminate and minimize defects. This will reduce the risk of failure, increase longevity, and reduce conflicts with vehicles.
- Increase planting space; make cutouts larger, meander sidewalks, and use structural soils to reduce future costs associated with infrastructure conflicts.
- Select species that are tolerant of harsh conditions and with a low potential to damage nearby pavement.
- Minimize competition from turf and weeds to encourage rapid establishment.

Figure 20—Trained volunteers can plant and maintain young trees, allowing the community to accomplish more at less cost and providing satisfaction for participants.

Where growing conditions are likely to be favorable, such as yard or garden settings, it may be cost-effective to use smaller, less expensive stock or bare-root trees. In highly urbanized settings and sites subject to vandalism, however, large stock may survive the initial establishment period better than small stock.

Use less expensive stock where appropriate

Develop standards of "establishment success" for different types of tree species. Perform periodic inspections to alert residents to tree health problems, and reward those whose trees meet your program's establishment standards. Replace dead trees as soon as possible, and identify ways to improve survivability.

Although organizing and training volunteers requires labor and resources, it is usually less costly than contracting the work. A cadre of trained volunteers can easily maintain trees until they reach a height of about 20 ft and limbs are too high to prune from the ground with pole pruners/saws. By the time trees reach this size, they are well established. Pruning during this establishment period should result in trees that will require less care in the long term. Training young trees can provide a strong branching structure that requires less structural and corrective pruning (Costello 2000). Ideally, young trees should be inspected and pruned every other year for the first 5 years after planting. Pruning thereafter, depending on species should occur about every 5 years to correct structural problems. For most trees, it's a good idea to maintain a single leader to height of no less than about 20 ft. This will facilitate clearance pruning of street trees to prevent conflicts with vehicles and reduce the potential for wind damage during storms and hurricanes.

Prune early

As trees grow larger, pruning costs may increase on a per-tree basis. The frequency of pruning will influence these costs, as it takes longer to prune a tree that has not been pruned in 10 years than one that has been pruned every 3 to 5 years, and it is less stressful to the tree. Specifications should be developed for tree pruning for each species and should emphasize structural development, not thinning or shaping. Although pruning frequency varies by species and location, a return frequency of about 5 to 8 years is usually sufficient for mature trees (Gilman 2002, Miller 1997).

Investing in the resources needed to promote tree establishment during the first 5 years after planting is usually worthwhile, because once trees are established they have a high probability of continued survival. If your program has targeted trees on private property, then encourage residents to attend tree-care workshops. These workshops should include information on recognizing pests and diseases and contact information for notifying authorities should an outbreak occur. Residents are an important first line of defense against pests in the Central Florida region, which is especially prone to attacks from nonnative species.

Match tree to site

Carefully select and locate trees to avoid conflicts with overhead power lines, sidewalks, and underground utilities. Time spent planning the planting will result in long-term savings. Also consider soil type and irrigation, microclimate, and the type of activities occurring around the tree that will influence its growth and management.

It all adds up—trees pay us back

When evaluating the bottom line, do not forget to consider tree services other than stormwater-runoff reductions, energy savings, atmospheric CO_2 reductions, and other tangible benefits. The magnitude of benefits related to employment opportunities, job training, community building, reduced violence, and enhanced

Figure 21—Trees pay us back in tangible and intangible ways.

human health and well-being can be substantial (fig. 21). Moreover, these benefits extend beyond the site where trees are planted, furthering collaborative efforts to build better communities.

For more information on urban and community forestry program design and implementation, see the list of additional resources in appendix 1.

USDA Forest Service, PSW, Center for Urban Forest Research

Chapter 5. General Guidelines for Selecting and Placing Trees

In this chapter, general guidelines for selecting and locating trees are presented. Residential trees and trees in public places are considered. In all cases, when selecting trees to maximize benefits, be sure to select species that are noninvasive to preserve native vegetation and natural ecosystems in Florida.

Guidelines for Energy Savings

Maximizing Energy Savings From Shading

The right tree in the right place can save energy and reduce tree care costs. The sun shines on the east side of a building in the morning, passes over the roof near midday, and then shines on the west side in the afternoon (fig. 4). Electricity use for cooling is highest during the afternoon when temperatures are warmest and incoming sunshine is greatest. Therefore, the west side of a home is the most important side to shade (Pandit and Laband, in press; Sand 1993) (fig. 22).

Depending on building orientation and window placement, sun shining through windows can heat a home quickly during the morning hours. The east side is the second most important side to shade when considering the net impact of tree shade on energy savings (fig. 22).

The closer a tree is to a home the more shade it provides, but roots of trees that are too close can damage the foundation. Branches too close to the building can make it difficult to maintain exterior walls and windows. In addition, trees with branches overhanging the roof will drop leaves and wood onto the roof. Overhanging branches and trees planted too closely can cause significant damage during hurricanes and tropical storms. In Central Florida communities in particular, where roofs are more likely to be flat, debris can accumulate and cause damage as it rots. Keep trees 10 ft or farther from the home, depending on mature crown spread, to

Where should shade trees be planted?

Figure 22—Locate trees to shade west and east windows. (Illustration from Sand 1993.)

NORTH

avoid these conflicts. Trees within 30 to 50 ft of the home most effectively shade windows and walls. Trees beyond 50 ft of the home do not effectively shade windows and walls. In fire-prone areas, conifers should not be planted within about 30 ft of a home. A few individual specimens, though, can be planted within 30 ft, assuming they are well maintained and sufficiently pruned up. The UF/IFAS Extension Web site has more information on Florida fire-wise landscaping (Doran et al. 2004).

Paved patios and driveways can become **heat sinks** that warm the home during the day. Shade trees can make them cooler and more comfortable spaces. If a home is equipped with an air conditioner, shading can reduce its energy use, but do not plant vegetation so close that it will obstruct the flow of air around the unit.

Plant only small-growing trees under overhead power lines, and avoid planting directly above underground water and sewer lines if possible. Contact your local utility company before planting to determine where underground lines are located and which tree species should not be planted below power lines.

Selecting Trees to Maximize Benefits

There are many choices

The ideal shade tree has a fairly dense, round crown with limbs broad enough to partially shade the roof. Given the same placement, a large tree will provide more shade than a small tree. Plant small trees where nearby buildings or power lines limit aboveground space. Columnar trees are appropriate in narrow side yards. Because the best location for shade trees is relatively close to the west and east sides of buildings, the most suitable trees will be strong and capable of resisting storm damage, disease, and pests (Sand 1994).

Picking the right tree

Drought and water conservation are major issues currently for Floridians. When selecting trees, low water-use species are preferable, but be sure to match the tree's water requirements with those of surrounding plants. Also, match the tree's maintenance requirements with the amount of care and the type of use different areas in the landscape receive. Tree species, for example, that drop fruit that can be a slip-and-fall problem should not be planted near paved areas that are frequently used by pedestrians. The University of Florida Tree Selector Web site offers information on well over 1,000 tree species and allows users to select trees based on tree and site attributes (see http://orb.at.ufl.edu/FloridaTrees/index.html). Check with your local landscape professional before selecting trees to make sure that they are well suited to the site's soil and climatic conditions.

Use the following practices to plant and manage trees strategically to maximize energy conservation benefits:

- Increase community-wide tree canopy, and target shade to streets, parking lots, and other paved surfaces, as well as air-conditioned buildings.
- Shade west- and east-facing windows and walls.
- Shade air conditioners, but do not obstruct airflow.
- Avoid planting trees too close to utilities and buildings.

Guidelines for Reducing Carbon Dioxide

Because trees in common areas and other public places may not shelter buildings from sun and wind and reduce energy use, carbon dioxide (CO_2) reductions are primarily due to sequestration. Fast-growing trees sequester more CO_2 initially than slow-growing trees, but this advantage can be lost if the fast-growing trees die at younger ages. Large trees have the capacity to store more CO_2 than smaller trees (fig. 23). Use the Center for Urban Forest Research Tree Carbon Calculator (CTCC) to compare sequestration rates for different tree species in this region

USDA Forest Service, PSW, Center for Urban Forest Research

Figure 23—Compared with small trees, large trees can store more carbon, filter more air pollutants, intercept more rainfall, and provide greater energy savings. Here, young Shumard oaks line a downtown Orlando street.

(http://www.fs.fed.us/ccrc/topics/urban-forests/ctcc/). To maximize CO_2 sequestration, select tree species that are well suited to the site where they will be planted. Consult resources such as *Plant Health Care for Woody Ornamentals: a Professional's Guide to Preventing and Managing Environmental Stresses and Pests* (Lloyd 1997), and, for information on abiotic disorders, refer to *Abiotic Disorders of Landscape Plants: a Diagnostic Guide* (Costello et al. 2003). Consult online resources at the Florida Division of Plant Industry (http://www.doacs.state.fl.us/pi/), University of Florida Landscape Plants (http://hort.ifas.ufl.edu/woody/index.shtml), University of Florida's Urban and Urbanizing Forestry program (http://www.sfrc.ufl.edu/urbanforestry/), and your local University of Florida Cooperative Extension Horticulture Advisors (http://edis.ifas.ufl.edu/topic_urban_forestry). Also consult landscape professionals and arborists to select the right tree for your site. Trees that are not well-adapted will grow slowly, show symptoms of stress, or die at an early age. Unhealthy trees do little to reduce atmospheric CO_2 and can be unsightly liabilities in the landscape.

Design and management guidelines that can increase CO_2 reductions include the following:

- Preserve existing tree cover.
- Maximize use of woody plants, especially trees, as they store more CO_2 than do palms, herbaceous plants, and grasses.
- Plant more trees where feasible, and immediately replace dead trees to compensate for CO_2 lost through removal.
- Create a diverse assemblage of habitats, with trees of different ages and species, to promote a continuous canopy cover over time. Do not rely on a few favored species such as live oaks. Diversity is a key to developing sustainable landscapes. New, introduced insect and disease pests are a constant threat to urban trees. It is also important to avoid species that are invasive and can spread in natural habitats.
- Consider the project's lifespan when selecting species. Although fast-growing species will sequester more CO_2 initially than slow-growing species, many are short-lived and begin to decline in 30 years or less.
- Avoid removing trees by considering other alternatives. Alternatives should include, but are not limited to:

  - Crown reduction to improve safety
  - Changing project design
  - Bridging over roots
  - Ramping sidewalks

- Using flexible paving materials or thinner sections
- Using permeable paving materials and enlarging tree wells (cutouts)
- Reducing sidewalk width

- Group species with similar landscape maintenance requirements together and consider how irrigation, pruning, fertilization, and weed, pest, and disease control can be minimized.
- Reduce CO_2 associated with landscape management by using push mowers (not gas or electric), hand saws (not chain saws), pruners (not gas/electric shears), rakes (not leaf blowers), and employ landscape professionals who don't have to travel far to your site.
- Reduce maintenance by reducing turfgrass and planting sustainable landscapes.
- Provide ample space belowground for tree roots to grow so that they can maximize CO_2 sequestration and tree longevity.
- When trees die or are removed, salvage as much wood as possible for use as furniture and other long-lasting products to delay decomposition or use as a bioenergy source.
- Plant trees, shrubs, and vines in strategic locations to maximize summer shade and reduce winter shade, thereby reducing atmospheric CO_2 emissions associated with power production.

Guidelines for Reducing Stormwater Runoff

Trees are mini-reservoirs, controlling runoff at the source because their leaves and branch surfaces intercept and store rainfall, thereby reducing runoff volumes and erosion of watercourses, as well as delaying the onset of peak flows. Rainfall interception by large trees is a relatively inexpensive first line of defense in the battle to control nonpoint-source pollution.

When selecting trees to maximize rainfall interception benefits, consider the following:

- Select tree species with physiological features that maximize interception, such as evergreen foliage, large leaf surface area, and rough surfaces that store water (Metro 2002).
- Increase interception by planting large trees where possible (fig. 24).
- Plant low-water-use tree species that, once established, require little supplemental irrigation.
- In bioretention areas, such as roadside swales, select species that tolerate inundation, are long-lived, wide-spreading, and fast-growing (Metro 2002).

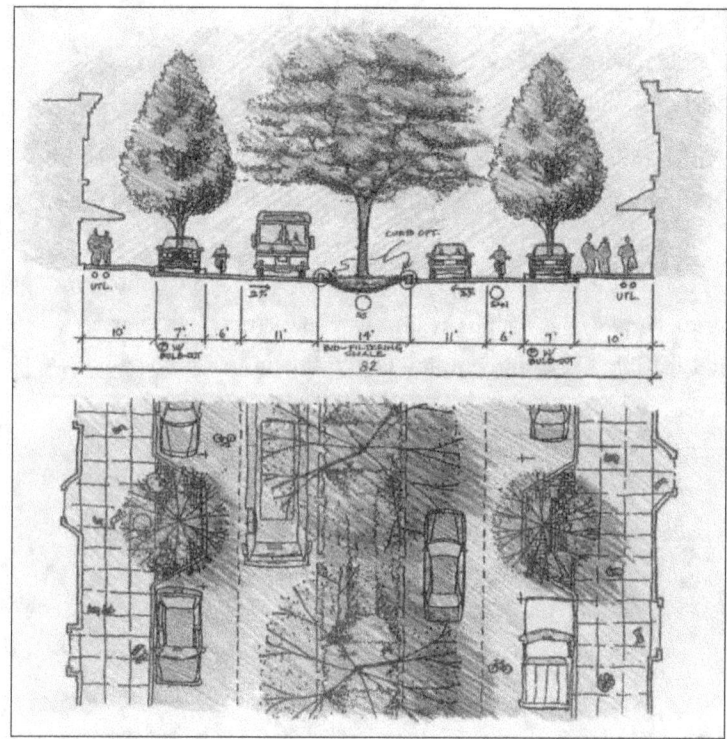

Figure 24—Trees can create a continuous canopy for maximum rainfall interception, even in commercial areas. In this example, a swale in the median filters runoff and provides ample space for large trees. Parking-space-sized planters contain the soil volume required to grow healthy, large trees. (Illustration from Metro 2002.)

- Along streets, sidewalks, and parking lots, plant trees in engineered soils designed to capture runoff from adjacent paving and promote deep root growth.
- Do not pave over streetside planting strips for easier weed control; this can impair tree health and increase runoff.
- Minimize compaction during construction activities.

Guidelines for Improving Air Quality Benefits

Trees, sometimes called the "lungs of our cities," are important because of their ability to remove contaminants from the air. The amount of gaseous pollutants and particulates removed by trees depends on their size and architecture, as well as local meteorology and pollutant concentrations.

Along streets, in parking lots, and in commercial areas, locate trees to maximize shade on paving and parked vehicles. Shade trees reduce heat that is stored or reflected by paved surfaces. By cooling streets and parking areas, trees reduce emissions of evaporative hydrocarbons from parked cars and thereby reduce smog formation (Scott et al. 1999). Large trees can shade a greater area than smaller trees, but should be used only where space permits.

Tree planting and management guidelines to improve air quality include the following (Nowak 2000, Smith and Dochinger 1976):

- It is important to allow adequate space for root growth to ensure long-term survival. Planting projects should emphasize large cutouts, wide planting strips, increasing space every time pavement must be repaired owing to root-pavement conflicts, and avoiding soil compaction where trees and landscapes are planned. Engineered soil mixes can also be used to facilitate root development in mass-graded sites and planting areas surrounded by pavement.

- Select species that tolerate pollutants that are present in harmful concentrations. For example, in areas with high ozone (O_3) concentration, avoid sensitive species such as sweetgum, red maple, and loblolly pine (Coulston et al. 2003).

- Broadleaf evergreens and conifers have high surface-to-volume ratios and retain their foliage year round, which may make them more effective than deciduous species.

- Species with long leaf stems and hairy plant parts are especially efficient interceptors.

- Effective uptake depends on proximity to the pollutant source and the amount of biomass. Where space and fire conditions permit, plant multilayered stands near the source of pollutants.

- Consider the local meteorology and topography to promote airflow that can "flush" pollutants out of the city along streets and greenspace corridors. Use columnar-shaped trees instead of spreading forms to avoid trapping pollutants under the canopy and obstructing airflow.

- In areas with unhealthy O_3 concentrations, maximize use of plants that emit low levels of biogenic volatile organic compounds to reduce ozone formation—for example, members of the pea family. Consider beneficial effects from large trees, such as urban heat island reduction and pollutant uptake, relative to their species-based biogenic volatile organic compound emissions.

- To reduce emissions of volatile organic compounds and other pollutants, plant trees to shade parked cars and conserve energy.

- Sustain large, healthy trees; they produce the most benefits.

Guidelines for Avoiding Conflicts With Infrastructure

Conflicts between trees and infrastructure create lose-lose situations. Examples include trees growing into power lines, blocking traffic signs, and roots heaving sidewalks. Trees lose because often they must be altered or removed to rectify the problem. People lose directly because of the additional expense incurred to eliminate the conflict. They lose indirectly owing to benefits foregone when a large tree is replaced with a smaller tree or, too frequently, no tree at all. Tree conflicts with infrastructure are usually avoidable with good planning and judicious tree selection. Tree Selector, a Web-based tree selection program contains a wealth of information on trees for the region (http://orb.at.ufl.edu/FloridaTrees/index.html). Guidelines to reduce conflicts with infrastructure include the following:

- Before planting, contact your local before-digging company, such as Call Before You Dig/Call 811, to locate underground water, sewer, gas, and telecommunications lines.
- Avoid locating trees where they will block streetlights or views of traffic and commercial signs.
- Check with local transportation officials for sight visibility requirements. Keep trees at least 30 ft away from street intersections to ensure visibility.
- Avoid planting shallow-rooting species near sidewalks, curbs, and paving. Tree roots can heave pavement if planted too close to sidewalks and patios. Generally, avoid planting within 3 ft of pavement, and remember that trunk flare at the base of large trees can displace soil and paving for a considerable distance. When space is limited, use smaller trees. Use strategies to reduce damage by tree roots such as meandering sidewalks around trees ramping sidewalks over tree roots, root barriers, and deflectors (Costello and Jones 2003).
- Select only small trees (<25 ft tall) under overhead power lines, and do not plant directly above underground water and sewer lines (fig. 25). Avoid locating trees where they will block illumination from streetlights or views of street signs in parking lots, commercial areas, and along streets.

For trees to deliver benefits over the long term, they require enough soil volume to grow and remain healthy. Matching tree species to the site's soil volume can reduce sidewalk and curb damage as well. Figure 26 shows recommended soil volumes for different size trees.

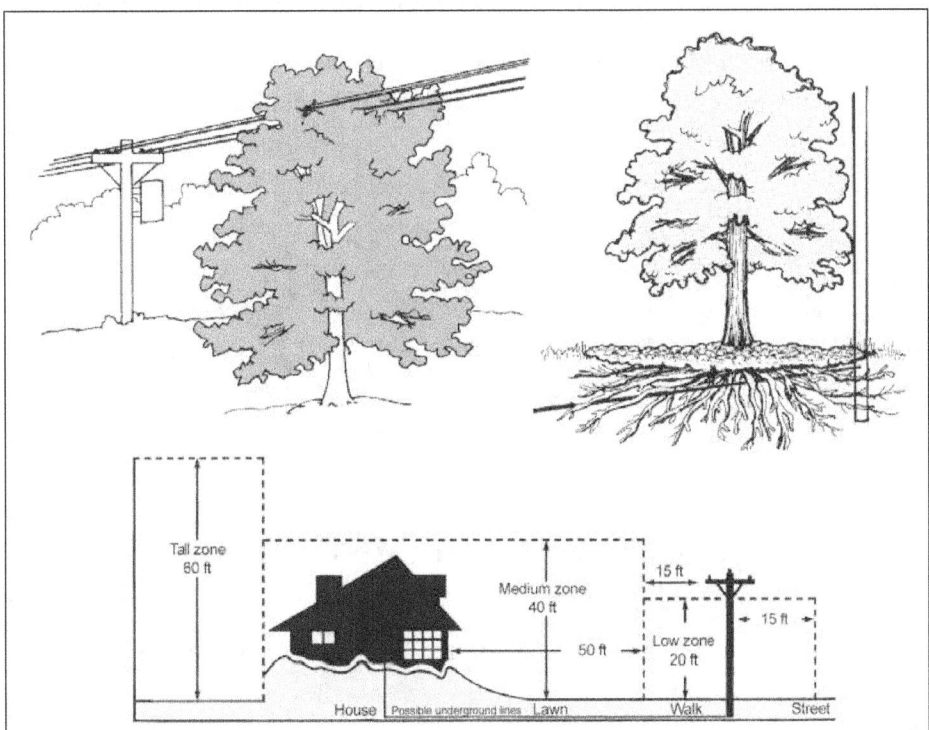

Figure 25—Know where power lines and other utility lines are before planting. Under power lines, use only small-growing trees ("low zone") and avoid planting directly above underground utilities. Larger trees may be planted where space permits ("medium" and "tall zones"). (Illustration from ISA 1992.)

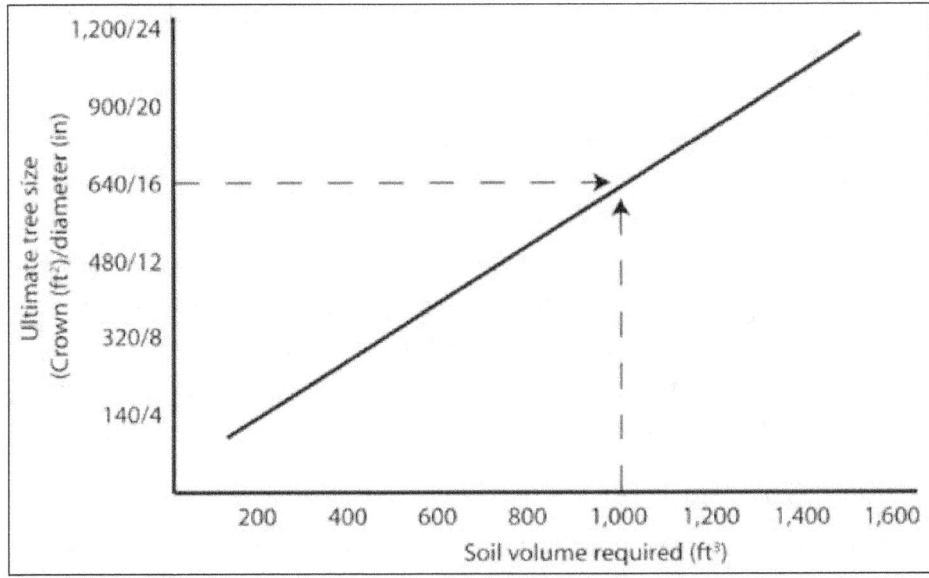

Figure 26—Developed from several sources by Urban (1992), this graph shows the relationship between tree size and required soil volume. For example, a tree with a 16-in diameter at breast height (41 cm) with 640 ft² of crown projection area (59.5 m² under the dripline) requires 1,000 ft³ (28 m³) of soil. (Illustration from Costello and Jones 2003.)

Maintenance requirements and public safety concerns influence the type of trees selected for public places. The ideal public tree is not susceptible to wind damage and branch drop, does not require frequent pruning, produces negligible litter, is deep-rooted, has few serious pest and disease problems, and tolerates a wide range of soil conditions, irrigation regimes, and air pollutants. Because relatively few trees have all these traits, it is important to match the tree species to the planting site by determining what issues are most important on a case-by-case basis. For example, parking-lot trees should be tolerant of hot, dry conditions, have strong branch attachments, and be resistant to attacks by pests that leave vehicles covered with sticky exudates. Check with your local horticulture extension agency, state urban forestry program, or city forestry department for horticultural information on tree traits.

Guidelines for Maximizing Long-Term Benefits
Invasive Nonnative Species

In the previous sections, we have offered suggestions for choosing trees to achieve certain goals. A basic underlying rule, however, must always be to choose species that are not, on balance, harmful to native vegetation and natural ecosystems. Special care should be taken when selecting nonnative plants to avoid those that are invasive species. Invasive species are plants that have been brought to a region for aesthetic or agricultural reasons or have been introduced accidentally and are able to gain a special foothold in their new environment. In Central Florida communities, they can destroy native ecosystems, displace native plants, and disturb habitats for native fauna.

Not all nonnative plant species are invasive; many have great economic or aesthetic value and pose little risk to their ecosystems. The difficulty lies in distinguishing between the two. The Florida Exotic Plant Pest Council (FLEPPC) publishes an annual list of species known to have caused or likely to cause ecological damage (FLEPPC 2009). The FLEPPC Web site (http://www.fleppc.org) has many other helpful references, including links to individual county resources on prohibited plants, scientific and general publications to provide more information, and ways to get involved in helping to combat the problem of invasive species.

Planting Guidelines

Selecting a tree from the nursery that has a high probability of becoming a healthy, low-maintenance, **mature tree** is critical to a successful outcome. Therefore, select the very best stock at your nursery, and when necessary, reject stock that does not meet industry standards. The University of Florida, Institute of Food and Agricultural Sciences Extension (2006b) and the Florida Division of Plant Industry (2009) provide a good starting point for communities interested in creating their own standards for nurseries or for assessing quality.

The health of the tree's root ball is critical to its ultimate survival. If the tree is in a container, check for matted or circling roots by sliding off the container. Roots should penetrate to the edge of the root ball, but not densely circle the inside of the container or grow through drain holes. As well, at least two large structural roots should emerge from the trunk within 1 to 3 in of the soil surface. If there are no roots in the upper portion of the root ball, excess soil has been placed over the top of the root ball, and the root ball that has developed is undersized or poorly formed. Such trees should be avoided.

The roots of containerized trees should be shaved (outer 1/2 to 1 in of the root ball trimmed away) carefully with a sharp blade or saw to ensure that roots will grow horizontally and radially outward into the backfill and native soil. In addition, the soil on top of the root ball should also be removed down to where the first main root originates. This will prevent deep planting and future rooting problems.

Another way to evaluate the quality of the tree before planting is to gently move the trunk back and forth. A good tree trunk bends and does not move in the soil, whereas a poor trunk bends a little and pivots at or below the soil line—a tell-tale sign of a poorly anchored tree. If the tree is balled-and-burlapped, be careful not to move the trunk too vigorously, as this could loosen the roots. It is also a good idea to remove the burlap or fold it down at least half way. Better yet, cut as much of it away as possible without disturbing the root ball.

A good tree is well-anchored

Dig the planting hole 1 in shallower than the depth of the root ball to allow for some settling after watering. Make the hole two to three times as wide as the root ball and loosen the sides of the hole to make it easier for roots to penetrate. Place the tree so that the root flare is at the top of the soil. If the structural roots have grown properly as described above, the top of the root ball will be slightly higher (1 to 2 in) than the surrounding soil to allow for settling. Backfill with the native soil unless it is very rocky or sandy, in which case you may want to add composted organic matter such as peat moss or shredded bark (fig. 27). Once the tree has been backfilled, loosen the surrounding soil with a shovel or digging bar to reduce compaction and encourage root growth.

Plant the tree in the right size hole

Planting trees in urban plazas, commercial areas, and parking lots poses special challenges because of limited soil volume and poor soil structure. Engineered soils and other soil volume expansion solutions can be placed under the **hardscape** to

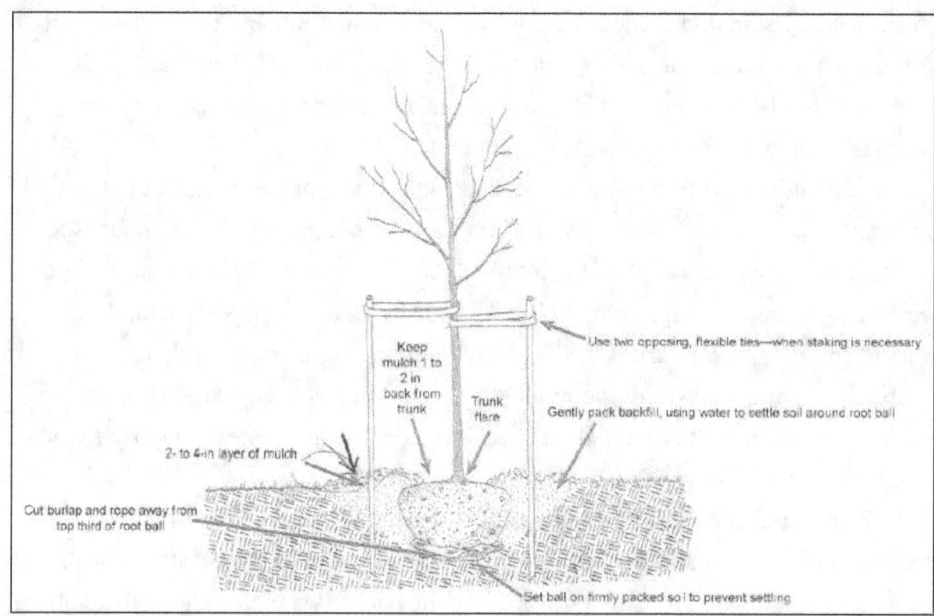

Figure 27—Prepare a broad planting area, plant the tree with the root flare at or just above ground level, and provide a berm/water ring to retain water (drawing courtesy of International Society of Arboriculture). (Note that trunk flare shown here represents a tree grown under optimum conditions. In trees grown under poorer conditions, the trunk flare may be hidden beneath the soil. These trees should be rejected in favor of those grown more carefully, or at the very least, the soil should be removed to expose the flare.) (Illustration from ISA 1992.)

increase rooting space while meeting engineering requirements. For more information on engineered soils see *Reducing Infrastructure Damage by Tree Roots: a Compendium of Strategies* (Costello and Jones 2003) and *Up By Roots* (Urban 2008).

Use additional soil to build a berm outside the root ball that is 6 in high and 3 ft in diameter. Soak the root ball, and gently rock it to settle it in. Apply water directly to the rootball, as water applied outside of the rootball typically will not readily move into the rootball owing to textural differences between the soil in the root ball and the backfill. Apply water to the backfill soil to encourage rooting there. Handle only the ball so the trunk is not loosened. Water the new tree three times a week until the tree is established. Water more frequently during very hot, dry, or windy weather. Generally, a tree requires about 1 in of water per week. Add 3 to 5 gals each watering for a 15-gal tree, and more for a larger size. A rain gauge or soil moisture sensor (tensiometer) can help determine tree watering needs, or contact your local cooperative extension agent or water conservancy district for recommendations. For more information on proper tree planting see *Planting and Establishing Trees* (Gilman and Sadowski 2007).

Water trees as needed to facilitate rapid establishment and rapid growth. Once established, water trees as needed to maintain reasonable growth and health.

After you've planted your tree, remember the following:

- Inspect your tree several times a year, and contact a certified arborist if problems develop.
- If your tree needed staking to keep it upright, remove the stake and ties after 1 year or as soon as the tree can hold itself up. The staking should allow some tree movement, as this movement sends hormones to the roots causing them to grow and create greater tree stability. It also promotes trunk taper and growth. It may be necessary to stake a tree for several years until it has developed sufficient caliper to resist vandalism. Trees that have been grown with lower laterals often don't need to be staked.
- Avoid removing lower lateral branches because they support rapid growth and help to develop taper.
- Reapply mulch and irrigate the tree as needed.
- Retain but shorten lower lateral branches during the first few years. Prune the young tree to maintain a central main trunk and equally spaced branches. For more information, see Costello (2000). As the tree matures, have it pruned by a certified arborist or other experienced professional to remove dead or damaged branches. For more information, see Costello (2000) and Gilman (2002).
- Retain or develop a single, dominant leader by careful structural pruning. Lateral branches should be kept to less than half the diameter of the trunk by pruning. This will prevent lower laterals from becoming dominant (competing with the leader) and ultimately interfering with traffic.

By keeping your tree healthy, you maximize its ability to produce shade, intercept rainfall, reduce atmospheric CO_2, and provide other benefits. For more information on tree selection, planting, establishment, and care, see the resources listed in appendix 1.

Trees for Hurricane-Prone Areas

In addition to the damage they cause to urban infrastructure, hurricanes can also have a significant impact on a city's green infrastructure. Trees may be uprooted, snapped, or may lose large branches. But hurricanes don't affect all trees or all tree species equally. A study in Florida after several hurricanes between 1995 and 2005 showed that some species stood a better chance of surviving (Duryea et al. 2007). Trees having the highest survival in winds included bald cypress, Southern magnolia, live oak, sweetgum, crapemyrtle, flowering dogwood, and sabal palm, all having greater than an 80 percent survival rate (see "Common and Scientific

Names" section). The least wind resistant with 60 percent or less survival were tulip poplar, Carolina laurelcherry, laurel oak, water oak, spruce, and sand and longleaf pines. Other studies have shown bald cypress to be extremely wind resistant (Ogden 1992).

When cities manage trees properly, urban forests can provide protection from high winds (Gilman et al. 2006). General suggestions for selecting and maintaining trees in hurricane-prone areas include:

- Plant species that are more wind resistant (see Wind Resistant Tree Species at http://edis.ifas.ufl.edu/pdffiles/EP/EP29100.pdf).
- Match recommended species to the local site conditions.
- Plant trees in groups or clusters where feasible (Duryea et al. 2007).
- Provide trees with plenty of room for roots to grow—they provide the anchor that holds the tree in place. Root pruning will greatly reduce stability.
- Plant a variety of species, ages, and layers of trees and shrubs to maintain diversity.
- Consider soil properties (soil depth, water table, and compaction).
- Choose trees that resist decay, hence recover well from wind damage.
- Prune trees appropriately to remove weak branches and improve structure (Gilman et al. 2008a, 2008b). (See UF/IFAS Extension 2006a for extensive information on pruning.) "Topping" and "lion-tailing" in particular reduce tree strength, raise the tree's center of gravity, and reduce its aerodynamics.
- Municipalities, utility companies, and others responsible for tree maintenance should draft standards for pruning and care to reduce hurricane-related damage.

For more information on hurricane recovery and planning for a wind-resistant urban forest, the UF/IFAS Extension provides an excellent resource in their *Urban Forest Hurricane Recovery Program Series* available via the Electronic Data Information Source. See appendix 1 for links.

Glossary of Terms

annual fuel utilization efficiency (AFUE)—A measure of space heating equipment efficiency defined as the fraction of energy output per energy input.

anthropogenic—Caused by humans.

biodiversity—The variety of life forms in a given area. Diversity can be categorized in terms of the number of species, the variety in the area's plant and animal communities, the genetic variability of the animals or plants, or a combination of these elements.

biogenic—Produced by living organisms.

biogenic volatile organic compounds (BVOCs)—Hydrocarbon compounds from vegetation (e.g., isoprene, monoterpene) that exist in the ambient air and contribute to the formation of smog or may themselves be toxic. Emission rates ($\mu g \cdot g^{-1} \cdot hr^{-1}$) used for this report follow Benjamin and Winer (1998):

> Common crapemyrtle—0.0 (isoprene); 0.0 (monoterpene)
> Southern magnolia—0.0 (isoprene); 5.9 (monoterpene)
> Live oak—20.2 (isoprene); 0.3 (monoterpene)
> Slash pine—0.0 (isoprene); 5.3 (monoterpene)

caliper—diameter of the trunk measured 6 in above the ground (up to 4-in caliper size) and 12 in above the ground for larger sizes. Used by the nursery industry in the sale of trees.

canopy—A layer or multiple layers of branches and foliage at the top or crown of a forest's trees.

canopy cover—The area of land surface that is covered by tree canopy, as seen from above.

climate—The average weather for a particular region and period (usually 30 years). Weather describes the short-term state of the atmosphere; climate is the average pattern of weather for a particular region. Climatic elements include precipitation, temperature, humidity, sunshine, wind velocity; phenomena such as fog, frost, and hailstorms; and other measures of weather.

climate effects—Impact on residential space heating and cooling (pounds of carbon dioxide [CO_2] per tree per year) from trees located more than 50 ft from a building owing to associated reductions in windspeeds and summer air temperatures.

community forests—The sum of all woody and associated vegetation in and around human settlements, ranging from small rural villages to metropolitan regions.

conifers—Cone-bearing trees or shrubs with needle-like leaves that usually retain their leaves during the winter.

contract rate—The percentage of residential trees cared for by commercial arborists; the proportion of trees for which a specific service (e.g., pruning or pest management) is contracted.

control costs—The marginal cost of preventing, controlling, or mitigating an impact.

crown—The branches and foliage at the top of a tree.

damage costs—The total estimated economic loss to society produced by an impact.

deciduous—Trees or shrubs that lose their leaves every fall.

diameter at breast height (d.b.h.)—The diameter of a tree outside the bark measured 4.5 ft above the ground on the uphill side (where applicable) of the tree.

dripline—The area beneath a tree marked by the outer edges of the branches.

emission factor—The rate of CO_2, nitrogen dioxide (NO_2), sulfur dioxide (SO_2), and small particulate matter (PM_{10}) output resulting from the consumption of electricity, natural gas, or any other fuel source.

evapotranspiration (ET)—The total loss of water by evaporation from the soil surface and by transpiration from plants, from a given area, and during a specified period.

evergreens—Trees or shrubs that are never entirely leafless. Evergreens may be broadleaved or coniferous (cone-bearing with needlelike leaves).

greenspace—Urban trees, forests, and associated vegetation in and around human settlements, ranging from small communities in rural settings to metropolitan regions.

hardscape—Paving and other impervious ground surfaces that reduce infiltration of water into the soil.

heat sinks—Paving, buildings, and other surfaces that store heat energy from the sun.

hourly pollutant dry deposition—Removal of gases from the atmosphere by direct transfer to natural surfaces and absorption of gases and particles by natural surfaces such as vegetation, soil, water, or snow.

interception—Amount of rainfall held on tree leaves and stem surfaces.

kWh (kilowatt-hour)—A unit of work or energy, measured as 1 kW (1,000 watts) of power expended for 1 hour.

leaf area index (LAI)—Total leaf area per unit area of crown if crown were projected in two dimensions.

leaf surface area (LSA)—Measurement of area of one side of a leaf or leaves.

mature tree—A tree that has reached a desired size or age for its intended use. Size, age, and economic maturity differ depending on the species, location, growing conditions, and intended use.

mature tree size—The approximate size of a tree 40 years after planting.

metric tonne—A measure of weight (abbreviated "t") equal to 1,000,000 grams (1000 kg) or 2,205 lb.

municipal forester—A person who manages public street and/or park trees (municipal forestry programs) for the benefit of the community.

MWh (megawatt-hour)—A unit of work or energy, measured as one megawatt (1,000,000 watts) of power expended for 1 hour. One MWh is equivalent to 3.412 MBtu.

nitrogen oxides (oxides of nitrogen, NO_x)—A general term for compounds of nitric oxide (NO), nitrogen dioxide (NO_2), and other oxides of nitrogen. Nitrogen oxides are typically created during combustion processes and are major contributors to smog formation and acid deposition. NO_2 may cause numerous adverse human health effects.

ozone (O_3)—A strong-smelling, pale blue, reactive toxic chemical gas consisting of three oxygen atoms. It is a product of the photochemical process involving the Sun's energy. Ozone exists in the upper layer of the atmosphere as well as at the Earth's surface. Ozone at the Earth's surface can cause numerous adverse human health effects. It is a major component of smog.

peak flow (or peak runoff)—The maximum rate of runoff at a given point or from a given area, during a specific period.

photosynthesis—The process in green plants of converting water and CO_2 into sugar with light energy; accompanied by the production of oxygen.

PM_{10} (particulate matter)—Major class of air pollutants consisting of tiny solid or liquid particles of soot, dust, smoke, fumes, and mists. The size of the particles (10 microns or smaller, about 0.0004 in or less) allows them to enter the air sacs (gas-exchange region) deep in the lungs where they may be deposited and cause adverse health effects. PM_{10} also reduces visibility.

reduced powerplant emissions—Reduced emissions of CO_2 or other pollutants that result from reductions in building energy use owing to the moderating effect of trees on climate. Reduced energy use for heating and cooling results in reduced demand for electrical energy, which translates into fewer emissions by powerplants.

resource unit (RU)—The value used to determine and calculate benefits and costs of individual trees. For example, the amount of air conditioning energy saved in kilowatt-hours per year per tree, air-pollutant uptake in pounds per year per tree, or rainfall intercepted in gallons per tree per year.

riparian habitats—Narrow strips of land bordering creeks, rivers, lakes, or other bodies of water.

seasonal energy efficiency ratio (SEER)—The total heat removed from an air-conditioned space during the annual cooling season, expressed in British thermal units, divided by the total electrical energy consumed by the air conditioner or heat pump during the same season, expressed in watt-hours.

sequestration—Annual net rate that a tree removes CO_2 from the atmosphere through the processes of photosynthesis and respiration (pounds of CO_2 per tree per year).

shade coefficient—The percentage of light striking a tree crown that is transmitted through gaps in the crown. This is the percentage of light that hits the ground.

shade effects—Impact on residential space heating and cooling (pounds of CO_2 per tree per year) from trees located within 50 ft of a building.

stem flow—Amount of rainfall that travels down the tree trunk and onto the ground.

sulfur dioxide (SO_2)—A strong-smelling, colorless gas that is formed by the combustion of fossil fuels. Powerplants, which may use coal or oil high in sulfur content, can be major sources of SO_2. Sulfur oxides contribute to the problem of acid deposition.

t—See metric tonne.

therm—A unit of heat equal to 100,000 British thermal units (BTUs) or 100 kBtu.

throughfall—Amount of rainfall that falls directly to the ground below the tree crown or drips onto the ground from branches and leaves.

transpiration—The loss of water vapor through the stomata of leaves.

tree or canopy cover—Within a specific area, the percentage covered by the crown of an individual tree or delimited by the vertical projection of its outermost perimeter; small openings in the crown are ignored. Used to express the relative importance of individual species within a vegetation community or to express the coverage of woody species.

tree litter—Fruit, flowers, leaves, twigs, and other debris shed by trees.

tree-related CO_2 emissions—CO_2 released when growing, planting, and caring for trees.

tree surface saturation storage capacity—The maximum volume of water that can be stored on a tree's leaves, stems, and bark. This part of rainfall stored on the canopy surface does not contribute to surface runoff during and after a rainfall event.

urban heat island—An area in a city where summertime air temperatures are 3 to 8 °F warmer than temperatures in the surrounding countryside. Urban areas are warmer for two reasons: (1) dark construction materials for roofs and asphalt absorb solar energy, and (2) few trees, shrubs, or other vegetation provide shade and cool the air.

volatile organic compounds (VOCs)—Hydrocarbon compounds that exist in the ambient air. VOCs contribute to the formation of smog or are themselves toxic. VOCs often have an odor. Some examples of VOCs are gasoline, alcohol, and the solvents used in paints.

watt-hour (Wh)—a unit of energy equivalent to 1 watt of power expended for 1 hour of time.

willingness to pay—The maximum amount of money an individual would be willing to pay for nonmarket, public goods and services provided by environmental amenities such as trees and forests rather than do without.

Common and Scientific Names[a]

Common name	Scientific name
American sycamore	*Platanus occidentalis* L.
Baldcypress	*Taxodium distichum* (L.) Rich.
Black cherry	*Prunus serotina* Ehrh.
Black oak	*Quercus velutine* Lam.
Blackgum	*Nyssa sylvatica* Marsh.
Camphor	*Cinnamomum camphora* (L.) J. Presl
Carolina laurelcherry	*Prunus caroliniana* Aiton.
Chinese elm	*Ulmus parvifolia* Jacq.
Chinese tallow	*Triadica sebifera* (L.) Small
Common crapemyrtle	*Lagerstroemia indica* L.
Flowering dogwood	*Cornus florida* L.
Golden raintree	*Koelreuteria elegans* (Seem.) A.C. Sm.
Laurel oak	*Quercus laurifolia* Michx.
Live oak	*Quercus virginiana* Mill.
Loblolly pine	*Pinus taeda* L.
Longleaf pine	*Pinus palustris* Mill.
Loquat	*Eriobotrya japonica* (Thunb.) Lindl.
Oak	*Quercus* spp.
Oriental arborvitae	*Platycladus orientalis* (L.) Franco
Poplar	*Populus* spp.
Queen palm	*Syagrus romanzoffiana* (Cham.) Glassman
Red maple	*Acer rubrum* L.
Sabal palm	*Sabal palmetto* (Walter) Lodd. ex Schult. & Schult. f.
Sand pine	*Pinus clausa* (Chapm. ex Engelm.) Vasey ex Sarg.
Shumard oak	*Quercus shumardii* Buckley
Slash pine	*Pinus elliottii* Engelm.
Southern magnolia	*Magnolia grandiflora* L.
Southern redcedar	*Juniperus virginiana* var. *silicicola* (Small) E. Murray
Southern red oak	*Quercus falcata* Michx.
Spruce pine	*Pinus glabra* Walter
Sweetgum	*Liquidambar styraciflua* L.
Sycamore	*Platanus* spp.
Tulip poplar	*Liriodendron tulipifera* L.
Water oak	*Quercus nigra* L.
Washington fan palm	*Washingtonia robusta* H. Wendl.
Wax myrtle	*Morella cerifera* (L.) Small

[a] This list provides the scientific names for species mentioned in the text. It is not intended to serve as a list of recommended plants for the region.

Metric Equivalents

When you know:	Multiply by:	To find:
Inch (in)	25,400	Microns (μ)
Inches (in)	25.4	Millimeters (mm)
Inches (in)	2.54	Centimeters (cm)
Feet (ft)	.305	Meters (m)
Square feet (ft^2)	.0929	Square meters (m^2)
Cubic feet (ft^3)	.0283	Cubic meters (m^3)
Cubic yards (yd^3)	.7646	Cubic meters (m^3)
Miles (mi)	1.61	Kilometers (km)
Acres (ac)	.405	Hectares (ha)
Acre-feet (ac-ft)	1.23×10^6	Hectare meters (ha-m)
Square miles (mi^2)	2.59	Square kilometers (km^2)
Gallons (gal)	.00378	Cubic meters (m^3)
Pounds (lb)	.454	Kilograms (kg)
Pounds per square foot (lb/ft^2)	4.882	Kilograms per square meter (kg/m^2)
Ounces (oz)	28.35	Grams (g)
Ounces (oz)	2.83×10^7	Micrograms (μg)
Tons (ton)	.907	Metric tonnes (t)
Thousand British thermal units (kBtu)	1.05	Megajoules (MJ)
Thousand British thermal units (kBtu)	.293	Kilowatt-hours (kWh)
Million British thermal units (mmBtu)	8.141	Megawatt-hours (MWh)
Watts (W)	10^6	Megawatts (MW)
Watt-hour (Wh)	10^9	Gigawatt-hours (GWh)
Fahrenheit (°F)	(F−32).55	Celsius (°C)

Acknowledgments

We are indebted to Timothy Broschat, Francisco Escobedo (University of Florida), and Charles Marcus (Florida Division of Forestry) for providing insightful reviews of this work.

We greatly appreciate the assistance provided by Denise Aldridge and Andrew Kittsley (Orlando Parks Division, Families, Parks, and Recreation Department, city of Orlando, Florida), with special thanks to and Kevin McCann and Katie Kulbaba (Streets and Stormwater Division, Public Works Department, city of Orlando, Florida); Scott Maco, Joseph Gregory, Aren Dottenwhy, Doak Marsco, Amanda Peter, and John Duncan (Davey Resource Group.)

We thank those who returned our many requests and calls for tree care expenditure information: Denise Aldridge and Andrew Kittsley (city of Orlando, Florida), Linda Beck (city of Tampa, Florida), Brian Dick (city of Lakeland, Florida), Bill Geiger (city of Brooksville, Florida), Alan Mayberry (city of Dunedin, Florida), Linda Seufert (city of St. Petersburg, Florida), John Harris (Earth Advisors), Sergio Vasquez (Central Florida Tree Services), and Ward Reasoner (Ward Reasoner & Sons Landscaping).

Additionally, Keith Cline (USDA Forest Service, State and Private Forestry) and Charles Marcus (Florida Division of Forestry) provided invaluable support for this project.

References

Akbari, H.; Davis, S.; Dorsano, S.; Huang, J.; Winnett, S., eds. 1992. Cooling our communities: a guidebook on tree planting and light-colored surfacing. Washington, DC: U.S. Environmental Protection Agency. 26 p.

Alliance for Community Trees. 2006. Tree by tree, street by street. http://actrees. org. (27 January 2007).

American Forests. 2007. Urban ecosystem analysis, Palm Beach County, Florida: calculating the value of nature. Washington, DC. 16 p.

Anderson, L.M.; Cordell, H.K. 1988. Residential property values improve by landscaping with trees. Southern Journal of Applied Forestry. 9: 162–166.

Andreu, M.G.; Friedman, M.H.; Landry, S.M.; Northrop, R.J. 2008. City of Tampa Urban Ecological Analysis 2006–2007. Final report to the city of Tampa, April 24, 2008. City of Tampa, Florida. http://edis.ifas.uff.edu/fr265. (14 May 2010).

Andreu, M.G.; Friedman, M.H.; Landry, S.M.; Northrop, R.J. 2009. Environmental services provided by Tampa's urban forest. http://edis.ifas.ufl.edu/fr266. (19 March 2010).

Bedker, P.J.; O'Brien, J.G.; Mielke, M.E. 1995. How to prune trees. NA-FR-01-95. [Newtown Square, PA]: U.S. Department of Agriculture, Forest Service, Northeastern Area State and Private Forestry. 28 p.

Bell, M.L.; McDermott, A.; Zeger, S.L.; Samet, J.M.; Dominici, F. 2004. Ozone and short-term mortality in 95 US urban communities. Journal of the American Medical Association. 292: 2372–2378.

Benjamin, M.T.; Winer, A.M. 1998. Estimating the ozone-forming potential of urban trees and shrubs. Atmospheric Environment. 32: 53–68.

Bernhardt, E.; Swiecki, T.J. 1993. The state of urban forestry in California: results of the 1992 California Urban Forest Survey. Sacramento: California Department of Forestry and Fire Protection. 51 p.

Bond, J. 2006. The inclusion of large-scale tree planting in a state implementation plan. Geneva, NY: Davey Resource Group. 56 p.

Bratkovich, S.M. 2001. Utilizing municipal trees: ideas from across the country. NA-TP-06-01. Newtown Square, PA: U.S. Department of Agriculture, Forest Service, Northeastern Area State and Private Forestry. 91 p.

Brenzel, K.N., ed. 2001. Sunset western garden book. 7th ed. Menlo Park, CA: Sunset Books, Inc. 768 p.

Broschat, T.K. 2010a. Palm nutrition and fertilization.

Broschat, T.K. 2010b. Reviewers re palms in tree guide. tkbr@ufl.edu. (4 March 2010).

Broschat, T.K.; Meerow, A.W. 2000. Ornamental palm horticulture. Florida: University of Florida Press. 400 p. http://edis.ifas.ufl.edu/topic_palm_nutrition (17 March 2010).

Cappiella, K.; Schueler, T.; Wright, T. 2005. Urban watershed forestry manual. Ellicott City, MD: Center for Watershed Protection. 138 p.

Cardelino, C.A.; Chameides, W.L. 1990. Natural hydrocarbons, urbanization, and urban ozone. Journal of Geophysical Research. 95(9): 13971–13979.

Chameides, W.L.; Lindsay, R.W.; Richardson, J.; Kiang, C.S. 1988. The role of biogenic hydrocarbons in urban photochemical smog: Atlanta as a case study. Science. 241: 1473–1475.

Climate Action Reserve. 2010. Urban forest project protocol v1.1. Los Angeles, CA: Climate Action Reserve. 103 p.

Cohen, J.E.; Small, C.; Mellinger, A.; Gallup, J.; Sachs, J. 1997. Estimates of coastal populations. Science. 278(5341): 1211–1212.

Cook, D.I. 1978. Trees, solid barriers, and combinations: alternatives for noise control. In: Proceedings of the national urban forestry conference. ESF Publ. 80-003. Syracuse, NY: State University of New York: 330–334.

Costello, L.R. 2000. Training young trees for structure and form. [Video] V99-A. Oakland, CA: University of California, Agriculture and Natural Resources, Communication Services Cooperative Extension Service.

Costello, L.R.; Jones, K.S. 2003. Reducing infrastructure damage by tree roots: a compendium of strategies. Cohasset, CA: Western Chapter of the International Society of Arboriculture. 119 p.

Costello, L.R.; Perry, E.J.; Matheny, N.P.; Henry, J.M.; Geisel, P.M. 2003. Abiotic disorders of landscape plants: a diagnostic guide. Publ. No. 3420. Oakland, CA: University of California Agriculture and Natural Resources. 242 p.

Coulston, J.W.; Smith, G.C.; Smith, W.D. 2003. Regional assessment of ozone sensitive tree species using bioindicator plants. Environmental Monitoring and Assessment. 83: 113–127.

Donovan, G.H.; Butry, D.T. 2008. Market based approaches to tree valuation. Arborist News. 17(4): 52–55.

Doran, J.D.; Randall, C.K.; Long, A.J. 2004. Fire in the wildland-urban interface: selecting and maintaining firewise plants for landscaping. http://edis. ifas.ufl.edu/fr147. (22 March 2010).

Duryea, M.L.; Kampf, E.; Littell, R.C. 2007. Hurricanes and the urban forest: I. Effects of Southeastern United States coastal plain tree species. Arboriculture and Urban Forestry. 33: 83–97.

Dwyer, J.F.; McPherson, E.G.; Schroeder, H.W.; Rowntree, R.A. 1992. Assessing the benefits and costs of the urban forest. Journal of Arboriculture. 18(5): 227–234.

Dwyer, M.C.; Miller, R.W. 1999. Using GIS to assess urban tree canopy benefits and surrounding greenspace distributions. Journal of Arboriculture. 25(2): 102–107.

Escobedo, F.J.; Luley, C.J.; Bond, J.; Staudhammer, C.; Bartel, C. 2009. Hurricane debris and damage assessment for Florida urban forests. Arboriculture & Urban Forestry. 35(2): 100–106.

Fazio, J.R. [N.d.]. Tree City USA Bulletin Series. Lincoln, NE: The National Arbor Day Foundation.

Florida Automated Weather Network. 2009. Hourly data for Apopka. http://fawn. ifas.ufl.edu/station.php?id=320. (29 August 2009).

Florida Division of Plant Industry. 2009. Grades and standards. http://www.fl-dpi. com/pubs.html. (3 February 2010).

Florida Exotic Plant Pest Council [FLEPPC]. 2009. 2009 list of invasive plant species. http://www.fleppc.org/list/09PlantListfinal.pdf. (22 March 2010).

Gilman, E.F. 1997. Trees for urban and suburban landscapes. Albany, NY: Delmar Publishing. 688 p.

Gilman, E.F. 2002. An illustrated guide to pruning. 2nd ed. Albany, NY: Delmar Publishing. 256 p.

Gilman, E.F.; Duryea, M.L.; Kampf, E.; Partin, T.J.; Delgado, A.; Lehtola, C.J. 2006. Assessing damage and restoring trees after a hurricane. http://edis. ifas.ufl.edu/EP291. (22 March 2010).

Gilman, E.F.; Grabosky, J.C.; Jones, S.; Harchick, C. 2008a. Effects of pruning dose and type on trunk movement in tropical storm winds. Arboriculture and Urban Forestry. 34(1): 13–19.

Gilman, E.F.; Masters, F.; Grabosky, J.C. 2008b. Pruning affects tree movement in hurricane force wind. Arboriculture and Urban Forestry. 34(1): 20–28.

Gilman, E.F.; Sadowski, L. 2007. Planting and establishing trees. Publication No. ENH 1061. http://edis.ifas.ufl.edu/pdffiles/EP/EP31400.pdf. (22 March 2010).

Gonzalez, S. 2004. Personal communication. Assistant maintenance superintendent, City of Vallejo, 111 Amador St., Vallejo, CA 94590.

Grant, R.H.; Heisler, G.M.; Goa, W. 2002. Estimation of pedestrian level UV exposure under trees. Photochemistry and Photobiology. 75(4): 369–376.

Guenther, A.B.; Monson, R.K.; Fall, R. 1991. Isoprene and monoterpene emission rate variability: observations with eucalyptus and emission rate algorithm development. Journal of Geophysical Research. 96: 10799–10808.

Guenther, A.B.; Zimmermann, P.R.; Harley, P.C.; Monson, R.K.; Fall, R. 1993. Isoprene and monoterpene emission rate variability: model evaluations and sensitivity analyses. Journal of Geophysical Research. 98: 12609–12617.

Hamburg, S.P.; Harris, N.; Jaeger, J.; Karl, T.R.; McFarland, M.; Mitchell, J.; Oppenheimer, M.; Santer, B.; Schneider, S.; Trenberth, K.; Wigley, T. 1997. Common questions about climate change. Nairobi, Kenya: United Nations Environment Programme, World Meteorological Organization. 22 p.

Hammer, T.T.; Coughlin, R.; Horn, E. 1974. The effect of a large urban park on real estate value. Journal of the American Institute of Planning. July: 274–275.

Hammond J.; Zanetto, J.; Adams, C. 1980. Planning solar neighborhoods. Sacramento, CA: California Energy Commission. 179 p.

Hargrave, R.; Johnson, G.R.; Zins, M.E. 2002. Planting trees and shrubs for long-term health. MI-07681-S. St. Paul, MN: University of Minnesota Extension Service. 12 p.

Harris, R.W.; Clark, J.R.; Matheny, N.P. 2003. Arboriculture. 4th ed. Englewood Cliffs, NJ: Regents/Prentice Hall. 592 p.

Hightshoe, G.L. 1988. Native trees, shrubs, and vines for urban and rural America. New York: Van Nostrand Reinhold. 832 p.

Hildebrandt, E.W.; Kallett, R.; Sarkovich, M.; Sequest, R. 1996. Maximizing the energy benefits of urban forestation. In: Proceedings of the ACEEE 1996 summer study on energy efficiency in buildings. Washington, DC: American Council for an Energy Efficient Economy: 121–131. Vol. 9.

Hoyt, R.S. 1998. Ornamental plants for SubCentral Florida regions. Anaheim, CA: Livingston Press. 510 p.

Hudson, B. 1983. Private sector business analogies applied in urban forestry. Journal of Arboriculture. 9(10): 253–258.

Hughes, N.J. 2008. The great clean air tree planting project report. Novato, CA: California Urban Forest Council. 60 p.

Hull, R.B. 1992. How the public values urban forests. Journal of Arboriculture. 18(2): 98–101.

Intergovernmental Panel on Climate Change [IPCC]. 2007. Climate change 2007: synthesis report. Contribution of working groups I, II and III to the fourth assessment report of the Intergovernmental Panel on Climate Change [Core Writing Team, Pachauri, R.K.; Reisinger, A., eds. Geneva, Switzerland: Intergovernmental Panel on Climate Change. 104 p.

International Society of Arboriculture [ISA]. 1992. Avoiding tree and utility conflicts. Savoy, IL. 4 p.

Jo, H.K.; McPherson, E.G. 1995. Carbon storage and flux in residential greenspace. Journal of Environmental Management. 45: 109–133.

Kaplan, R. 1992. Urban forestry and the workplace. In: Gobster, P.H., ed. Managing urban and high-use recreation settings. Gen. Tech. Rep. NC-163. St. Paul, MN: U.S. Department of Agriculture, Forest Service, North Central Research Station: 41–45.

Kaplan, R.; Kaplan, S. 1989. The experience of nature: a psychological perspective. Cambridge, United Kingdom: Cambridge University Press. 360 p.

Kittsley, A. 2009. Phenology table. Andy.Kittsley@ci.orlando.fl.us (7 May).

Kruger, M. 2009. Hourly concentrations. Merle.Kruger@ocfl.net (22 April).

Lewis, C.A. 1996. Green nature/human nature: the meaning of plants in our lives. Chicago: University of Illinois Press. 176 p.

Lloyd, J. 1997. Plant health care for woody ornamentals: a professional's guide to preventing and managing environmental stresses and pests. Urbana-Champaign, IL: University of Illinois, College of Agriculture. 223 p.

Luley, C.J.; Bond, J. 2002. A plan to integrate management of urban trees into air quality planning. Naples, NY: Davey Resource Group. 61 p.

Maco, S.E.; McPherson, E.G. 2003. A practical approach to assessing structure, function, and value of street tree populations in small communities. Journal of Arboriculture. 29(2): 84–97.

Markwardt, L.J. 1930. Comparative strength properties of woods grown in the United States. Tech. Bull. 158. Washington, DC: U.S. Department of Agriculture. 38 p.

McCann, K. 2009. Stormwater management costs. Kevin.McCann@ CityofOrlando.net.

McHale, M.; McPherson, E.G.; Burke, I.C. 2007. The potential of urban tree plantings to be cost effective in carbon credit markets. Urban Forestry and Urban Greening. 6: 49–60.

McHale, M.R.; Burke, I.C.; Lefsky, M.A.; Peper, P.J.; McPherson, E.G. 2009. Urban forest biomass estimates: Is it important to use allometric relationships developed specifically for urban trees? Urban Ecosystems. 12: 95–113.

McPherson, E.G. 1984. Planting design for solar control. In: McPherson, E.G., ed. Energy-conserving site design. Washington, DC: American Society of Landscape Architects: 141–164. Chapter 8.

McPherson, E.G. 1992. Accounting for benefits and costs of urban greenspace. Landscape and Urban Planning. 22: 41–51.

McPherson, E.G. 1993. Evaluating the cost effectiveness of shade trees for demand-side management. The Electricity Journal. 6(9): 57–65.

McPherson, E.G. 1995. Net benefits of healthy and productive forests. In: Bradley, G.A., ed. Urban forest landscapes: integrating multidisciplinary perspectives. Seattle, WA: University of Washington Press: 180–194.

McPherson, E.G. 1998. Atmospheric carbon dioxide reduction by Sacramento's urban forest. Journal of Arboriculture. 24(4): 215–223.

McPherson, E.G. 2000. Expenditures associated with conflicts between street tree root growth and hardscape in California. Journal of Arboriculture. 26(6): 289–297.

McPherson, E.G. 2001. Sacramento's parking lot shading ordinance: environmental and economic costs of compliance. Landscape and Urban Planning. 57: 105–123.

McPherson, E.G.; Mathis, S., eds. 1999. Proceedings of the Best of the West summit. Sacramento, CA: Western Chapter, International Society of Arboriculture. 93 p.

McPherson, E.G.; Muchnick, J. 2005. Effects of tree shade on asphalt concrete pavement performance. Journal of Arboriculture. 31(6): 303–309.

McPherson, E.G.; Nowak, D.J.; Heisler, G.; Grimmond, S.; Souch, C.; Grant, R.; Rowntree, R.A. 1997. Quantifying urban forest structure, function, and value: Chicago's Urban Forest Climate Project. Urban Ecosystems. 1: 49–61.

McPherson, E.G.; Nowak, D.J.; Rowntree, R.A. 1994. Chicago's urban forest ecosystem: results of the Chicago Urban Forest Climate Project. Gen. Tech. Rep. NE-186. Radnor [Newtown Square], PA: U.S. Department of Agriculture, Forest Service, Northeastern Research Station. 201 p.

McPherson, E.G.; Peper, P.J. 1995. Infrastructure repair costs associated with street trees in 15 cities. In: Watson, G.W.; Neely, D., eds. Trees and building sites. Champaign, IL: International Society of Arboriculture: 49–63.

McPherson, E.G.; Sacamano, P.L.; Wensman, S. 1993. Modeling benefits and costs of community tree plantings. Albany, CA: U.S. Department of Agriculture, Forest Service, Pacific Southwest Research Station. 170 p.

McPherson, E.G.; Simpson, J.R. 1999. Carbon dioxide reduction through urban forestry: guidelines for professional and volunteer tree planters. Gen. Tech. Rep. PSW-171. Albany, CA: U.S. Department of Agriculture, Forest Service, Pacific Southwest Research Station. 237 p.

McPherson, E.G.; Simpson, J.R. 2002. A comparison of municipal forest benefits and costs in Modesto and Santa Monica, CA, USA. Urban Forestry and Urban Greening. 1: 61–74.

McPherson, E.G.; Simpson, J.R. 2003. Potential energy savings in buildings by an urban tree planting programme in California. Urban Forestry and Urban Greening. 2(2): 73–86.

McPherson, E.G.; Simpson, J.R.; Peper, P.J.; Gardner, S.L.; Vargas, K.E.; Maco, S.E.; Xiao, Q. **2006a.** Coastal Plain community tree guide: benefits, costs, and strategic planting. Gen. Tech. Rep. PSW-GTR-201. Albany, CA: U.S. Department of Agriculture, Forest Service, Pacific Southwest Research Station. 99 p.

McPherson, E.G.; Simpson, J.R.; Peper, P.J.; Gardner, S.L.; Vargas, K.E.; Maco, S.E.; Xiao, Q. **2006b.** Piedmont community tree guide: benefits, costs, and strategic planting. Gen. Tech. Rep. PSW-GTR-200. Albany, CA: U.S. Department of Agriculture, Forest Service, Pacific Southwest Research Station. 95 p.

McPherson, E.G.; Simpson, J.R.; Peper, P.J.; Gardner, S.L.; Vargas, K.E.; Xiao, Q. **2007.** Northeast community tree guide: benefits, costs, and strategic planting. Gen. Tech. Rep. PSW-GTR-202. Albany, CA: U.S. Department of Agriculture, Forest Service, Pacific Southwest Research Station. 106 p.

McPherson, E.G.; Simpson, J.R.; Peper, P.J.; Maco, S.E.; Gardner, S.L.; Cozad, S.K.; Xiao, Q. **2006c.** Midwest community tree guide: benefits, costs, and strategic planting. Gen. Tech. Rep. PSW-GTR-199. Albany, CA: U.S. Department of Agriculture, Forest Service, Pacific Southwest Research Station. 85 p.

McPherson, E.G.; Simpson, J.R.; Peper, P.J.; Maco, S.E.; Xiao, Q.; Hoefer, P.J. **2003.** Northern mountain and prairie community tree guide: benefits, costs, and strategic planting. Albany, CA: U.S. Department of Agriculture, Forest Service, Pacific Southwest Research Station. 88 p.

McPherson, E.G.; Simpson, J.R.; Peper, P.J.; Maco, S.E.; Xiao, Q.; Mulrean, E. **2004.** Desert southwest community tree guide: benefits, costs, and strategic planting. Albany, CA: U.S. Department of Agriculture, Forest Service, Pacific Southwest Research Station. 65 p.

McPherson, E.G.; Simpson, J.R.; Peper, P.J.; Scott, K.; Xiao, Q. **2000.** Tree guidelines for coastal southern California communities. Sacramento, CA: Local Government Commission. 97 p.

McPherson, E.G.; Simpson, J.R.; Peper, P.J.; Xiao, Q. **1999a.** Benefit-cost analysis of Modesto's municipal urban forest. Journal of Arboriculture. 25(5): 235–248.

McPherson, E.G.; Simpson, J.R.; Peper, P.J.; Xiao, Q. 1999b. Tree guidelines for San Joaquin Valley communities. Sacramento, CA: Local Government Commission. 63 p.

Metro. 2002. Green streets: innovative solutions for stormwater and stream crossings. Portland, OR: 144 p.

Miller, R.W. 1997. Urban forestry: planning and managing urban greenspaces. 2nd ed. Upper Saddle River, NJ: Prentice-Hall. 502 p.

More, T.A.; Stevens, T.; Allen, P.G. 1988. Valuation of urban parks. Landscape and Urban Planning. 15: 139–152.

Morgan, R. 1993. A technical guide to urban and community forestry. Portland, OR: World Forestry Center. 49 p.

National Association of Realtors. 2009. Metropolitan area existing-home prices. http://www.realtor.org/research/research/metroprice. (4 May 2009).

National Oceanic and Atmospheric Administration. 2007. http://cdo.ncdc.noaa.gov/qclcd/QCLCD. (6 August 2009).

Neely, D., ed. 1988. Valuation of landscape trees, shrubs, and other plants. 7th ed. Urbana, IL: International Society of Arboriculture. 50 p.

Nowak, D.J. 2000. Tree species selection, design, and management to improve air quality. In: Scheu, D.L., ed. 2000 ASLA annual meeting proceedings. Washington, DC: American Society of Landscape Architects: 23–27.

Nowak, D.J.; Civerolo, K.L.; Rao, S.T.; Sistla, G.; Luley, C.J.; Crane, D.E. 2000. A modeling study of the impact of urban trees on ozone. Atmospheric Environment. 34: 1601–1613.

Nowak, D.J.; Crane, D.E. 2002. Carbon storage and sequestration by urban trees in the USA. Environmental Pollution. 116(3): 381–389.

Nowak, D.J.; Crane, D.E.; Stevens, J.C. 2006. Air pollution removal by urban trees and shrubs in the United States. Urban Forestry and Urban Greening. 4(2006): 115–123.

Ogden, J.C. 1992. The impact of Hurricane Andrew on the ecosystems of south Florida. Conservation Biology. 6: 488–490.

Orlando Utilities Commission. 2009. OUC electric rates index rate schedules. http://www.ouc.com/en/residential/electric_and_water_rates/electric_rates.aspx. (13 March 2009).

Ottinger, R.L.; Wooley, D.R.; Robinson, N.A.; Hodas, D.R.; Babb, S.E. 1990. Environmental costs of electricity. New York: Oceana Publications. 769 p.

Pandit, R.; Laband, D.N. [In press]. Energy savings from tree shade. Ecological Economics (2010), DOI: 10.1016/j.ecolecon.2010.01.009.

Parsons, R.; Tassinary, L.G.; Ulrich, R.S.; Hebl, M.R.; Grossman-Alexander, M. 1998. The view from the road: implications for stress recovery and immunization. Journal of Environmental Psychology. 18(2): 113–140.

Pearce, D. 2003. The social cost of carbon and its policy implications. Oxford Review of Public Policy. 19(3): 362–384.

Peoples Gas. 2009. Index of rate schedules. http://www.peoplesgas.com/data/files/tariff/TariffSect7.pdf. (13 March 2009).

Peper, P.J.; McPherson, E.G. 2003. Evaluation of four methods for estimating leaf area of isolated trees. Urban Forestry and Urban Greening. 2(1): 19–29.

Peper, P.J.; McPherson, E.G.; Simpson, J.R.; Vargas, K.E.; Xiao, Q. 2009a. Northeast community tree guide: benefits, costs, and strategic planting. Gen Tech. Rep. PSW-GTR-219. Albany, CA: U.S. Department of Agriculture, Forest Service, Pacific Southwest Research Station. 115 p.

Peper, P.J.; McPherson, E.G.; Simpson, J.R.; Xiao, Q. 2009b. City of Orlando, Florida municipal forest resource analysis. Albany, CA: U.S. Department of Agriculture, Forest Service, Pacific Southwest Research Station. 58 p.

Pillsbury, N.H.; Reimer, J.L.; Thompson, R.P. 1998. Tree volume equations for fifteen urban species in California. Tech. Rep. 7. San Luis Obispo, CA: Urban Forest Ecosystems Institute, California Polytechnic State University. 56 p.

Platt, R.H.; Rowntree, R.A.; Muick, P.C., eds. 1994. The ecological city. Boston, MA: University of Massachusetts. 292 p.

Pokorny, J.D. 2003. Urban tree risk management: a community guide to program design and implementation. NA-TP-03-03. Newtown Square, PA: U.S. Department of Agriculture, Forest Service, Northeastern Area State and Private Forestry. [Pages unknown].

Randrup, T.B.; McPherson, E.G.; Costello, L.R. 2001. Tree root intrusion in sewer systems: review of extent and costs. Journal of Infrastructure Systems. 7: 26–31.

Richards, N.A.; Mallette, J.R.; Simpson, R.J.; Macie, E.A. 1984. Residential greenspace and vegetation in a mature city: Syracuse, New York. Urban Ecology. 8: 99–125.

Rosenzweig, C.; Solecki, W.; Parshall, L.; Gaffin, S.; Lynn, B.; Goldberg, R.; Cox, J.; Hodges, S. 2006. Mitigating New York City's heat island with urban forestry, living roofs, and light surfaces. http://ams.confex.com/ams/pdfpapers/103341.pdf. (14 May 2008).

Sand, M. 1993. Energy saving landscapes: the Minnesota homeowner's guide. Minneapolis, MN: Minnesota Department of Natural Resources. [Pages unknown].

Sand, M. 1994. Design and species selection to reduce urban heat island and conserve energy. In: Proceedings from the 6th national urban forest conference: growing greener communities. Washington, DC: American Forests. 282 p.

Sarkovich, M. 2009. Personal communication. Program manager, Sacramento Municipal Utility District, 6301 S St., MS 4A23, Sacramento, CA 95852.

Schroeder, H.W.; Cannon, W.N. 1983. The esthetic contribution of trees to residential streets in Ohio towns. Journal of Arboriculture. 9: 237–243.

Schroeder, T. 1982. The relationship of local park and recreation services to residential property values. Journal of Leisure Research. 14: 223–234.

Scott, K.I.; McPherson, E.G.; Simpson, J.R. 1998. Air pollutant uptake by Sacramento's urban forest. Journal of Arboriculture. 24(4): 224–234.

Scott, K.I.; Simpson, J.R.; McPherson, E.G. 1999. Effects of tree cover on parking lot microclimate and vehicle emissions. Journal of Arboriculture. 25(3): 129–142.

Simpson, J.R. 1998. Urban forest impacts on regional space conditioning energy use: Sacramento County case study. Journal of Arboriculture. 24(4): 201–214.

Smith, W.H. 1990. Air pollution and forests. New York: Springer-Verlag. 618 p.

Smith, W.H.; Dochinger, L.S. 1976. Capability of metropolitan trees to reduce atmospheric contaminants. In: Santamour, F.S.; Gerhold, H.D.; Little, S., eds. Better trees for metropolitan landscapes. Gen. Tech. Rep. NE-22. Upper Darby [Newtown Square], PA: U.S. Department of Agriculture, Forest Service, Northeastern Research Station: 49–60.

Sullivan, W.C.; Kuo, E.E. 1996. Do trees strengthen urban communities, reduce domestic violence? Arborist News. 5(2): 33–34.

Summit, J.; McPherson, E.G. 1998. Residential tree planting and care: a study of attitudes and behavior in Sacramento, California. Journal of Arboriculture. 24(2): 89–97.

Sydnor, T.D.; Gamstetter, D.; Nichols, J.; Bishop, B.; Favorite, J.; Blazer, C.; Turpin, L. 2000. Trees are not the root of sidewalk problems. Journal of Arboriculture. 26: 20–29.

Taha, H. 1996. Modeling impacts of increased urban vegetation on ozone air quality in the South Coast Air Basin. Atmospheric Environment. 30: 3423–3430.

Thompson, R.P.; Ahern, J.J. 2000. The state of urban and community forestry in California. San Luis Obispo, CA: Urban Forest Ecosystems Institute, California Polytechnic State University. 48 p.

Tol, R.S.J. 2005. The marginal damage costs of carbon dioxide emissions: an assessment of the uncertainties. Energy Policy: 33: 2064–2074.

Tretheway, R.; Manthe, A. 1999. Skin cancer prevention: another good reason to plant trees. In: McPherson, E.G.; Mathis, S., eds. Proceedings of the Best of the West summit. Davis, CA: University of California: 72–75.

Tschantz, B.A.; Sacamano, P.L. 1994. Municipal tree management in the United States. Kent, OH: Davey Resource Group.

Tyrvainen, L. 1999. Monetary valuation of urban forest amenities in Finland. Res. Pap. 739. Vantaa, Finland: Finnish Forest Research Institute. 129 p.

Ulrich, R.S. 1985. Human responses to vegetation and landscapes. Landscape and Urban Planning. 13: 29–44.

United States Government [U.S. Government]. 2010. Diversity map. http://www.recovery.gov/Transparency/RecipientReportedData/Pages/RecipientReportedDataMap.aspx?datasource=diversity. (18 March 2010).

University of Florida Institute of Food and Agricultural Sciences Extension [UF IFAS Extension]. 2006a. Landscape plants: pruning shade trees in the landscape. http://hort.ifas.ufl.edu/woody/pruning/index.htm. (26 January 2010).

University of Florida Institute of Food and Agricultural Sciences Extension [UF IFAS Extension]. 2006b. Producing quality trees. http://hort.ifas.ufl.edu/woody/nursery_production.html. (26 January 2010).

Urban, J. 1992. Bringing order to the technical dysfunction within the urban forest. Journal of Arboriculture. 18(2): 85–90.

Urban, J. 2008. Up by roots: healthy soils and trees in the built environment. Champaign, IL: International Society of Arboriculture. 479 p.

Urban Horticulture Institute. 2003. Recommended urban trees: site assessment and tree selection for stress tolerance. http://www.hort.cornell.edu/UHI/outreach/recurbtree/index.html. (7 February 2007).

U.S. Department of Agriculture, Natural Resource Conservation Service [USDA NRCS]. 2005. Working trees for treating waste. Agroforestry Center. Western Arborist. 31: 50–52.

U.S. Department of Agriculture, Soil Conservation Service [USDA SCS]. 1986. Urban hydrology for small watersheds. Technical Release 55. 2nd ed. Washington, DC. 164 p.

U.S. Department of Commerce, Bureau of the Census. 2009. Population finder for 2008 estimates. http://factfinder.census.gov/home/saff/main.html?_lang=eng. (May 2009).

U.S. Environmental Protection Agency [US EPA]. 1998. Compilation of air pollutant emission factors. AP42. 5th ed. Research Triangle Park, NC. Volume I. [Pages unknown.]

U.S. Environmental Protection Agency [US EPA]. 2006a. Air quality system reports. http://www.epa.gov/air/data/reports.html. (21 November 2006).

U.S. Environmental Protection Agency [US EPA]. 2006b. E-GRID (E-GRID2006 Edition). http://www.epa.gov/cleanenergy/egrid/index.htm. (6 December 2006).

U.S. Environmental Protection Agency [US EPA]. 2010. Reducing urban heat islands: a compendium of strategies: trees and vegetation. http://www.epa.gov/heatisland/resources/pdf/TreesandVegCompendium.pdf. (23 March 2010).

Vargas, K.E.; McPherson, E.G.; Simpson, J.R.; Peper, P.J.; Gardner, S.L.; Xiao, Q. 2007a. Interior West community tree guide: benefits, costs, and strategic planting. Gen Tech. Rep. PSW-GTR-205. Albany, CA: U.S. Department of Agriculture, Forest Service, Pacific Southwest Research Station. 105 p.

Vargas, K.E.; McPherson, E.G.; Simpson, J.R.; Peper, P.J.; Gardner, S.L.; Xiao, Q. 2007b. Temperate Interior West community tree guide: benefits, costs, and strategic planting. Gen Tech. Rep. PSW-GTR-206. Albany, CA: U.S. Department of Agriculture, Forest Service, Pacific Southwest Research Station. 108 p.

Wang, M.Q.; Santini, D.J. 1995. Monetary values of air pollutant emissions in various U.S. regions. Transportation Research Record. 1475: 33–41.

Watson, G.W.; Himelick, E.B. 1997. Principles and practice of planting trees and shrubs. Savoy, IL: International Society of Arboriculture. 199 p.

Wolf, K.L. 2007. The environmental psychology of shopping: assessing the value of trees. Research Review. 14(3): 39–43.

Xiao, Q.; McPherson, E.G. 2002. Rainfall interception by Santa Monica's municipal urban forest. Urban Ecosystems. 6: 291–302.

Xiao, Q.; McPherson, E.G.; Simpson, J.R.; Ustin, S.L. 1998. Rainfall interception by Sacramento's urban forest. Journal of Arboriculture. 24(4): 235–244.

Xiao, Q.; McPherson, E.G.; Simpson, J.R.; Ustin, S.L. 2000. Winter rainfall interception by two mature open grown trees in Davis, California. Hydrological Processes. 14(4): 763–784.

USDA Forest Service, PSW, Center for Urban Forest Research

Appendix 1: Additional Resources

Additional information regarding urban and community forestry program design and implementation can be obtained from the following sources:

Utilizing Municipal Trees: Ideas From Across the Country by S.M. Bratkovich (2001)

Urban Forestry: Planning and Managing Urban Greenspaces by R.W. Miller (1997)

A Technical Guide to Urban and Community Forestry by R. Morgan (1993)

Urban Tree Risk Management: A Community Guide to Program Design and Implementation edited by J.D. Pokorny (2003)

For additional information on tree selection, planting, establishment, and care, see the following resources:

How to Prune Trees by P.J. Bedker, J.G. O'Brien, and M.E. Mielke (1995)

Training Young Trees for Structure and Form, a video by L.R. Costello (2000)

An Illustrated Guide to Pruning by E.F. Gilman (2002)

Trees for Urban and Suburban Landscapes by E.F. Gilman (1997)

Ornamental Palm Horticulture by T.K. Broschat and A.W. Meerow (2000)

Planting Trees and Shrubs for Long-Term Health by R. Hargrave, G.R. Johnson, and M.E. Zins (2002)

Arboriculture, 4th ed., by R.W. Harris, J.R. Clark, and N.P. Matheny (2003)

Native Trees, Shrubs, and Vines for Urban and Rural America by G.L. Hightshoe (1988)

Ornamental Plants for Subtropical Regions by R.S. Hoyt (1998)

Principles and Practice of Planting Trees and Shrubs by G.W. Watson and E.B. Himelick (1997)

Alliance for Community Trees: http://actrees.org (2006)

International Society of Arboriculture: http://www.isa-arbor.com

National Arbor Day Foundation: http://www.arborday.org

TreeLink: http://www.treelink.org

The Urban Horticulture Institute: http://www.hort.cornell.edu/UHI/outreach/recurbtree/index.html (2003)

State urban forestry agency and Web site for the Central Florida region:

Florida Division of Forestry, Urban and Community Forestry, 3125 Conner Blvd., Suite R3, Tallahassee, FL 32399; Phone: 850-921-0300; http://fl-dof.com/forest_management/cfe_urban_index.html

University of Florida-IFAS EDIS Urban Forest Hurricane Recovery Program series: http://edis.ifas.ufl.edu/topic_series_urban_forest_hurricane_recovery_program

University of Florida-IFAS Assessing Damage and Restoring Trees After a Hurricane: http://edis.ifas.ufl.edu/pdffiles/EP/EP29100.pdf

University of Florida-IFAS Landscape Plants (Edward F. Gilman): http://hort.ufl.edu/woody/

University of Florida-IFAS Palm nutrition and fertilization (Timothy K. Broschat): http//:edis.ifas.ufl.edu/topic_palm_nutrition

University of Florida's Urban and Urbanizing Forests Program: http://www.sfrc.ufl.edu/urbanforestry/

University of Florida IFAS Urban forestry extension publications: http://edis.ifas.ufl.edu/topic_urban_forestry

These suggested references are only a starting point. Your local cooperative extension agent, urban forester, or state forestry agency can provide you with up-to-date and local information.

Appendix 2: Benefit–Cost Information Tables

Information in this appendix can be used to estimate benefits and costs associated with proposed tree plantings. The tables contain data for representative small (common crapemyrtle), medium (southern magnolia), large (live oak) trees, and a large conifer (slash pine) (see "Common and Scientific Names" section). Data are presented as annual values for each 5-year interval after planting (tables 6 to 17). Annual values incorporate effects of tree loss. Based on the results of our survey, we assume that 40 percent of the trees planted die by the end of the 40-year period.

For the benefits tables (tables 6, 9, 12, and 15), there are two columns for each 5-year interval. In the first column, values describe **resource units** (RUs): for example, the amount of air conditioning energy saved in kilowatt-hours per year per tree, air pollutant uptake in pounds per year per tree, and rainfall intercepted in gallons per year per tree. Energy and carbon dioxide (CO_2) benefits for residential yard trees are broken out by tree location to show how shading effects differ among trees opposite west-, south-, and east-facing building walls. The second column for each 5-year interval contains dollar values obtained by multiplying RUs by local prices (e.g., kWh saved [RU] x $/kWh).

In the costs tables (tables 7, 10, 13, and 16), costs are broken down into categories for yard and public trees. Costs for yard trees do not differ by planting location (i.e., east, west, south walls). Although tree purchase and planting costs occur at year 1, we divided this value by 5 years to derive an average annual cost for the first 5-year period. All other costs are the estimated values for each year and not values averaged over 5 years.

Annual net benefits are calculated by subtracting annual costs from annual benefits and are presented in tables 8, 11, 14, and 17. Data are presented for a yard tree opposite west-, south-, and east-facing walls, as well as for the public tree.

The last column in each table presents 40-year-average annual values. These numbers were calculated by dividing the total costs and benefits by 40 years.

Table 6—Annual benefits at 5-year intervals and 40-year average for a representative small tree (crapemyrtle)

Benefits/tree	Year 5 RU	Value	Year 10 RU	Value	Year 15 RU	Value	Year 20 RU	Value	Year 25 RU	Value	Year 30 RU	Value	Year 35 RU	Value	Year 40 RU	Value	40-year average RU	Value
		Dollars		*Dollars*		*Dollars*		*Dollars*		*Dollars*		*Dollars*		*Dollars*		*Dollars*		*Dollars*
Cooling (kWh):																		
Yard: west	23	3.06	55	7.30	80	10.57	100	13.20	106	14.02	103	13.60	96	12.66	89	11.72	82	10.77
Yard: south	9	1.22	24	3.15	36	4.74	46	6.05	49	6.49	48	6.31	45	5.87	41	5.44	37	4.91
Yard: east	19	2.51	47	6.15	70	9.18	89	11.69	95	12.51	92	12.16	86	11.32	80	10.48	72	9.50
Public	7	0.90	15	1.95	21	2.78	27	3.50	28	3.74	28	3.63	26	3.38	24	3.13	22	2.88
Heating (kBtu):																		
Yard: west	2	0.01	4	0.01	5	0.01	5	0.01	6	0.02	6	0.01	5	0.01	5	0.01	5	0.01
Yard: south	2	0.01	2	0.01	3	0.01	3	0.01	2	0.01	2	0.01	2	0.01	2	0.005	2	0.01
Yard: east	-2	0	-3	-0.01	-4	-0.01	-4	-0.01	-3	-0.01	-3	-0.01	-3	-0.01	-3	-0.01	-3	-0.01
Public	4	0.01	8	0.02	12	0.03	14	0.04	15	0.04	15	0.04	14	0.04	13	0.03	12	0.03
Net energy (kBtu):																		
Yard: west	234	3.06	557	7.31	806	10.58	1,006	13.21	1,069	14.04	1,037	13.61	966	12.67	894	11.74	821	10.78
Yard: south	95	1.22	241	3.16	362	4.75	462	6.06	494	6.49	480	6.31	447	5.88	414	5.44	375	4.91
Yard: east	189	2.51	463	6.14	693	9.17	883	11.68	946	12.50	919	12.15	856	11.31	792	10.47	718	9.49
Public	72	0.91	157	1.97	223	2.81	280	3.54	299	3.78	290	3.67	270	3.42	250	3.16	230	2.91
Net carbon dioxide (lb):																		
Yard: west	65	0.22	155	0.52	231	0.77	266	0.89	271	0.90	266	0.89	258	0.86	250	0.83	220	0.74
Yard: south	37	0.12	91	0.30	141	0.47	156	0.52	154	0.51	153	0.51	153	0.51	152	0.51	130	0.43
Yard: east	56	0.19	136	0.45	209	0.70	242	0.81	246	0.82	243	0.81	237	0.79	230	0.77	200	0.67
Public	32	0.11	73	0.24	112	0.37	118	0.39	113	0.38	113	0.38	116	0.39	118	0.39	99	0.33
Air pollution (lb):[a]																		
Ozone uptake	0.0967	0.21	0.2064	0.45	0.3082	0.68	0.3996	0.88	0.4478	0.98	0.4964	1.09	0.5499	1.21	0.5951	1.31	0.39	0.85
Nitrous oxide uptake + avoided	0.0483	0.11	0.1145	0.25	0.1686	0.37	0.2137	0.47	0.2297	0.50	0.2276	0.50	0.2185	0.48	0.2087	0.46	0.18	0.39
Sulfur dioxide uptake + avoided	0.0337	0.07	0.0812	0.16	0.1194	0.24	0.1509	0.30	0.1613	0.32	0.1571	0.32	0.1471	0.30	0.1369	0.27	0.12	0.25
Small particulate matter uptake + avoided	0.0158	0.03	0.0585	0.12	0.1105	0.23	0.1735	0.36	0.2208	0.46	0.2622	0.55	0.2576	0.54	0.2530	0.53	0.17	0.36
Volatile organic compounds avoided	0.0144	0.01	0.0346	0.04	0.0509	0.05	0.0643	0.07	0.0686	0.07	0.0667	0.07	0.0621	0.06	0.0575	0.06	0.05	0.05
Biogenic volatile organic compounds released	0	0	0	0	0	0	0	0	0	0	0	0	0	0	0	0	0	0
Avoided + net uptake	0.209	0.43	0.495	1.03	0.758	1.57	1.002	2.08	1.128	2.35	1.210	2.53	1.235	2.59	1.251	2.63	0.91	1.90
Hydrology (gal):																		
Rainfall interception	242	0.73	610	1.83	1,101	3.30	1,749	5.25	2,130	6.39	2,251	6.75	2,251	6.75	2,251	6.75	1,573	4.72
Aesthetics and other benefits:																		
Yard		9.00		13.51		17.49		9.95		10.36		10.63		10.78		10.79		11.56
Public		10.20		15.31		19.82		11.28		11.74		12.05		12.21		12.23		13.10
Total benefits:																		
Yard: west		13.44		24.20		33.72		31.38		34.03		34.41		33.65		32.74		29.70
Yard: south		11.50		19.83		27.58		23.86		26.10		26.73		26.50		26.12		23.53
Yard: east		12.86		22.96		32.23		29.76		32.42		32.87		32.22		31.41		28.34
Public		12.38		20.39		27.88		22.54		24.63		25.37		25.36		25.17		22.96

Note: Annual values incorporate effects of tree loss. We assume that 5 percent of trees planted die during the first 5 years, 35 percent during the remaining 35 years, for a total mortality of 40 percent.
RU = resource unit.
[a] Values are the same for yard and public trees.

Table 7—Annual costs (dollars per tree) at 5-year intervals and 40-year average for a representative small tree (crapemyrtle)

Costs	Year 5	Year 10	Year 15	Year 20	Year 25	Year 30	Year 35	Year 40	40-year average
					Dollars				
Tree and planting:[a]									
Yard	88.00								11.00
Public	46.00								5.75
Pruning:									
Yard	0.07	0.02	1.18	1.09	1.01	0.92	0.84	0.75	0.73
Public	1.90	3.60	9.56	9.00	8.44	7.88	7.31	6.75	6.83
Remove and dispose:									
Yard	4.14	4.22	5.54	6.47	7.40	9.33	9.26	10.19	6.36
Public	1.57	2.79	3.66	4.28	4.89	5.51	6.12	6.73	4.13
Pest and disease:									
Yard	0.09	0.15	0.19	0.20	0.22	0.22	0.22	0.22	0.18
Public	0.10	0.17	0.20	0.22	0.24	0.25	0.26	0.27	0.20
Infrastructure repair:									
Yard	0.09	0.14	0.18	0.19	0.20	0.21	0.21	0.21	0.17
Public	0.73	1.23	1.53	1.68	1.80	1.89	1.95	1.98	1.51
Irrigation:									
Yard	0.04	0.07	0.08	0.09	0.09	0.10	0.10	0.10	0.08
Public	0	1.90	0	0	0	0	0	0	0.24
Cleanup:									
Yard	0.04	0.07	0.08	0.09	0.09	0.10	0.10	0.10	0.08
Public	0.34	0.58	0.72	0.79	0.85	0.89	0.92	0.93	0.71
Liability and legal:									
Yard	0.01	0.02	0.02	0.02	0.02	0.02	0.02	0.02	0.02
Public	0.08	0.13	0.16	0.18	0.19	0.20	0.21	0.21	0.16
Admin/inspect/other:									
Yard	0.56	0.93	1.13	1.23	1.29	1.33	1.34	1.33	1.09
Public	1.37	2.31	2.86	3.15	3.37	3.55	3.66	3.72	2.84
Total costs:									
Yard	93.00	5.55	8.32	9.30	10.23	11.13	11.99	12.81	19.63
Public	53.98	10.81	18.70	19.30	19.78	20.16	20.43	20.59	22.39

Note: Annual values incorporate effects of tree loss. We assume that 5 percent of trees planted die during the first 5 years, 35 percent during the remaining 35 years, for a total mortality of 40 percent.
[a] Although tree and planting costs occur in year 1, this value was divided by 5 years to derive an average annual cost for the first 5-year period.

Table 8—Annual net benefits (dollars per tree) at 5-year intervals and 40-year average for a representative small tree (crapemyrtle)

Total net benefits	Year 5	Year 10	Year 15	Year 20	Year 25	Year 30	Year 35	Year 40	40-year average
					Dollars				
Yard: west	-80	19	25	22	24	23	22	20	10
Yard: south	-81	14	19	15	16	16	15	13	4
Yard: east	-80	17	24	20	22	22	20	19	9
Public	-42	10	9	3	5	5	5	5	1

Note: Annual values incorporate effects of tree loss. We assume that 5 percent of trees planted die during the first 5 years, 35 percent during the remaining 35 years, for a total mortality of 40 percent.

See table 6 for annual benefits and table 7 for annual costs.

96

Table 9—Annual benefits (dollars per tree) at 5-year intervals and 40-year average for a representative medium tree (southern magnolia)

Benefits/tree	Year 5		Year 10		Year 15		Year 20		Year 25		Year 30		Year 35		Year 40		40-year average	
	RU	Value	RU	Value	RU	Value	RU	Value	RU	Value	RU	Value	RU	Value	RU	Value	RU	Value
		Dollars		Dollars		Dollars		Dollars		Dollars		Dollars		Dollars		Dollars		Dollars
Cooling (kWh):																		
Yard: west	28	3.67	86	11.34	140	18.39	186	24.49	224	29.48	249	32.76	262	34.50	268	35.29	180	23.74
Yard: south	10	1.29	37	4.89	73	9.60	106	13.92	134	17.61	156	20.58	171	22.52	180	23.77	108	14.27
Yard: east	22	2.88	73	9.61	126	16.58	171	22.54	205	27.03	230	30.35	245	32.30	250	32.92	165	21.78
Public	6	0.76	17	2.26	30	3.98	42	5.53	52	6.87	61	8.08	68	8.92	73	9.59	44	5.75
Heating (kBtu):																		
Yard: west	-1	0	-4	-0.01	-5	-0.01	-6	-0.01	-4	-0.01	-2	-0.01	-1	0.00	0	0.00	-3	-0.01
Yard: south	-1	0	-10	-0.03	-30	-0.08	-47	-0.13	-59	-0.16	-69	-0.19	-76	-0.20	-80	-0.21	-46	-0.12
Yard: east	-6	-0.02	-11	-0.03	-11	-0.03	-10	-0.03	-7	-0.02	-4	-0.01	-1	0.00	0	0.00	-6	-0.02
Public	3	0.01	9	0.03	15	0.04	21	0.06	26	0.07	30	0.08	32	0.09	33	0.09	21	0.06
Net energy (kBtu):																		
Yard: west	278	3.67	856	11.33	1,390	18.38	1,853	24.48	2,233	29.47	2,483	32.76	2,616	34.49	2,677	35.29	1,798	23.73
Yard: south	96	1.28	361	4.86	699	9.52	1,009	13.79	1,276	17.45	1,492	20.40	1,633	22.32	1,723	23.56	1,036	14.15
Yard: east	213	2.86	718	9.58	1,247	16.55	1,700	22.51	2,044	27.02	2,299	30.34	2,449	32.29	2,498	32.92	1,646	21.76
Public	61	0.77	181	2.29	317	4.02	441	5.59	547	6.94	643	8.16	708	9.00	761	9.68	457	5.81
Net carbon dioxide (lb):																		
Yard: west	70	0.23	210	0.70	346	1.16	468	1.56	573	1.91	655	2.19	711	2.38	663	2.21	462	1.54
Yard: south	33	0.11	110	0.37	207	0.69	299	1.00	383	1.28	459	1.53	517	1.73	476	1.59	311	1.04
Yard: east	57	0.19	182	0.61	317	1.06	437	1.46	534	1.78	618	2.06	677	2.26	627	2.09	431	1.44
Public	26	0.09	71	0.24	125	0.42	178	0.59	227	0.76	278	0.93	320	1.07	270	0.90	187	0.62
Air pollution (lb):[a]																		
Ozone uptake	0.1166	0.26	0.3128	0.69	0.5509	1.21	0.7912	1.74	1.0233	2.25	1.2853	2.82	1.5291	3.36	1.7811	3.91	0.92	2.03
Nitrous oxide uptake + avoided	0.0550	0.12	0.1741	0.38	0.3016	0.66	0.4159	0.91	0.5116	1.12	0.5899	1.30	0.6436	1.41	0.6814	1.50	0.42	0.93
Sulfur dioxide uptake + avoided	0.0382	0.08	0.1239	0.25	0.2143	0.43	0.2938	0.59	0.3587	0.72	0.4079	0.82	0.4384	0.88	0.4556	0.91	0.29	0.58
Small particulate matter uptake + avoided	0.0195	0.04	0.0859	0.18	0.2006	0.42	0.3607	0.76	0.5085	1.07	0.6713	1.41	0.8308	1.75	0.9855	2.07	0.46	0.96
Volatile organic compounds avoided	0.0160	0.02	0.0524	0.05	0.0906	0.09	0.1241	0.13	0.1511	0.16	0.1713	0.18	0.1833	0.19	0.1896	0.20	0.12	0.13
Biogenic volatile organic compounds released	-0.014	-0.01	-0.264	-0.27	-0.609	-0.63	-1.213	-1.25	-1.876	-1.94	-2.787	-2.88	-3.886	-4.02	-5.162	-5.33	-1.98	-2.04
Avoided + net uptake	0.232	0.50	0.485	1.28	0.749	2.19	0.773	2.87	0.677	3.38	0.339	3.64	-0.261	3.57	-1.069	3.25	0.24	2.59
Hydrology (gal):																		
Rainfall interception	1,212	3.64	2,145	6.44	3,333	10.00	4,657	13.97	6,226	18.68	8,361	25.08	10,471	31.41	13,124	39.37	6,191	18.57
Aesthetics and other benefits:																		
Yard		20.23		24.26		27.73		30.66		33.04		34.88		36.16		14.19		27.73
Public		22.93		27.49		31.43		34.75		37.45		39.52		40.98		16.89		31.43
Total benefits:																		
Yard: west		28.27		44.00		59.45		73.55		86.48		98.55		108.02		95.03		74.17
Yard: south		25.76		37.20		50.13		62.30		73.82		85.54		95.20		82.67		64.08
Yard: east		27.42		42.17		57.53		71.48		83.90		96.01		105.70		92.54		72.09
Public		27.92		37.73		48.05		57.77		67.20		77.34		86.04		70.10		59.02

Note: Annual values incorporate effects of tree loss. We assume that 5 percent of trees planted die during the first 5 years, 35 percent during the remaining 35 years, for a total mortality of 40 percent.

RU = resource unit.

[a] Values are the same for yard and public trees.

Table 10—Annual costs (dollars per tree) at 5-year intervals and 40-year average for a representative medium tree (southern magnolia)

Costs	Year 5	Year 10	Year 15	Year 20	Year 25	Year 30	Year 35	Year 40	40-year average
					Dollars				
Tree and planting:[a]									
Yard	88.00								11.00
Public	46.00								5.75
Pruning:									
Yard	0.07	1.26	1.18	1.09	1.01	3.69	3.34	3.00	1.58
Public	1.90	10.13	9.56	9.00	8.44	12.25	11.38	10.50	8.54
Remove and dispose:									
Yard	4.30	4.40	6.35	8.29	10.24	12.18	14.13	15.64	8.58
Public	1.63	2.91	4.20	5.48	6.77	8.05	9.34	10.34	5.60
Pest and disease:									
Yard	0.10	0.16	0.22	0.26	0.30	0.33	0.34	0.34	0.24
Public	0.10	0.17	0.23	0.29	0.33	0.37	0.40	0.41	0.27
Infrastructure repair:									
Yard	0.09	0.15	0.20	0.24	0.28	0.30	0.29	0.32	0.22
Public	0.76	1.28	1.75	2.15	2.49	2.76	2.97	3.04	2.01
Irrigation:									
Yard	0	0	0	0	0	0	0	0	0
Public	0	1.90	0.00	0.00	0.00	0.00	0.00	0.00	0.24
Cleanup:									
Yard	0.04	0.07	0.10	0.12	0.13	0.14	0.14	0.15	0.11
Public	0.36	0.61	0.83	1.01	1.17	1.30	1.40	1.43	0.95
Liability and legal:									
Yard	0.01	0.02	0.02	0.13	0.03	0.03	0.03	0.03	0.02
Public	0.08	0.14	0.19	0.23	0.27	0.30	0.32	0.33	0.22
Admin/inspect/other:									
Yard	0.58	0.97	1.30	1.57	1.79	1.95	1.86	2.04	1.44
Public	1.42	2.41	3.28	4.03	4.67	5.19	5.58	5.71	3.78
Total costs:									
Yard	93.18	7.03	9.36	11.61	13.77	18.62	20.13	21.51	23.20
Public	54.14	17.65	20.04	22.20	24.14	30.22	31.39	31.75	27.37

Note: Annual values incorporate effects of tree loss. We assume that 5 percent of trees planted die during the first 5 years, 35 percent during the remaining 35 years, for a total mortality of 40 percent.
[a] Although tree and planting costs occur in year 1, this value was divided by 5 years to derive an average annual cost for the first 5-year period.

Table 11—Annual net benefits (dollars per tree) at 5-year intervals and 40-year average for a representative medium tree (southern magnolia)

Total net benefits	Year 5	Year 10	Year 15	Year 20	Year 25	Year 30	Year 35	Year 40	40-year average
					Dollars				
Yard: west	-65	37	50	62	73	80	88	74	51
Yard: south	-67	30	41	51	60	67	75	61	41
Yard: east	-66	35	48	60	70	77	86	71	49
Public	-26	20	28	36	43	47	55	38	32

Note: Annual values incorporate effects of tree loss. We assume that 5 percent of trees planted die during the first 5 years, 35 percent during the remaining 35 years, for a total mortality of 40 percent.
See table 9 for annual benefits and table 10 for annual costs.

Table 12—Annual benefits (dollars per tree) at 5-year intervals and 40-year average for a representative large tree (live oak)

Benefits/tree	Year 5 RU	Year 5 Value	Year 10 RU	Year 10 Value	Year 15 RU	Year 15 Value	Year 20 RU	Year 20 Value	Year 25 RU	Year 25 Value	Year 30 RU	Year 30 Value	Year 35 RU	Year 35 Value	Year 40 RU	Year 40 Value	40-year average RU	40-year average Value
		Dollars		Dollars		Dollars		Dollars		Dollars		Dollars		Dollars		Dollars		Dollars
Cooling (kWh):																		
Yard: west	69	9.14	175	23.08	271	35.69	339	44.67	387	51.02	418	55.05	431	56.88	437	57.61	316	41.64
Yard: south	32	4.19	96	12.71	168	22.11	227	29.89	274	36.12	309	40.75	336	44.27	352	46.43	224	29.56
Yard: east	59	7.79	160	21.08	250	32.99	317	41.74	364	47.97	393	51.85	407	53.65	414	54.55	296	38.95
Public	14	1.88	38	5.04	65	8.63	91	11.95	114	15.01	135	17.85	152	20.06	167	21.99	97	12.80
Heating (kBtu):																		
Yard: west	-3	-0.01	-5	-0.01	-3	-0.01	-1	0.00	2	0.01	4	0.01	7	0.02	-15	-0.04	-2	0.00
Yard: south	-12	-0.03	-42	-0.11	-79	-0.21	-110	-0.29	-132	-0.35	-143	-0.38	-151	-0.40	-152	-0.41	-103	-0.27
Yard: east	-9	-0.02	-9	-0.02	-4	-0.01	2	0.01	7	0.02	13	0.03	18	0.05	21	0.06	5	0.01
Public	8	0.02	20	0.05	32	0.09	42	0.11	50	0.13	55	0.15	58	0.16	60	0.16	41	0.11
Net energy (kBtu):																		
Yard: west	691	9.13	1,746	23.07	2,704	35.68	3,388	44.67	3,872	51.03	4,180	55.06	4,321	56.90	4,355	57.57	3,157	41.64
Yard: south	306	4.16	922	12.59	1,598	21.90	2,158	29.60	2,608	35.77	2,949	40.37	3,208	43.87	3,370	46.02	2,140	29.28
Yard: east	582	7.77	1,590	21.05	2,499	32.98	3,168	41.74	3,647	47.99	3,946	51.88	4,088	53.70	4,160	54.61	2,960	38.97
Public	151	1.91	403	5.09	687	8.72	948	12.06	1,188	15.14	1,410	18.00	1,580	20.21	1,728	22.15	1,012	12.91
Net carbon dioxide (lb):																		
Yard: west	189	0.63	477	1.59	765	2.56	1,006	3.36	1,210	4.04	1,382	4.62	1,522	5.08	1,650	5.51	1,025	3.42
Yard: south	111	0.37	313	1.04	547	1.83	764	2.55	964	3.22	1,144	3.82	1,308	4.37	1,461	4.88	826	2.76
Yard: east	167	0.56	446	1.49	724	2.42	960	3.21	1,163	3.89	1,333	4.45	1,473	4.92	1,607	5.37	984	3.29
Public	78	0.26	202	0.67	351	1.17	505	1.69	659	2.20	813	2.72	959	3.20	1,109	3.70	584	1.95
Air pollution (lb):[a]																		
Ozone uptake	0.233	0.51	0.624	1.37	1.121	2.46	1.654	3.63	2.206	4.84	2.770	6.09	3.341	7.34	3.954	8.68	1.99	4.37
Nitrous oxide uptake+ avoided	0.141	0.31	0.378	0.83	0.617	1.36	0.813	1.79	0.973	2.14	1.100	2.42	1.195	2.63	1.274	2.80	0.81	1.78
Sulfur dioxide uptake + avoided	0.101	0.20	0.272	0.55	0.439	0.88	0.568	1.14	0.668	1.34	0.741	1.49	0.788	1.58	0.819	1.64	0.55	1.10
Small particulate matter uptake + avoided	0.051	0.11	0.169	0.36	0.369	0.78	0.651	1.37	0.943	1.98	1.232	2.59	1.511	3.18	1.822	3.83	0.84	1.77
Volatile organic compounds avoided	0.043	0.04	0.116	0.12	0.186	0.19	0.239	0.25	0.280	0.29	0.309	0.32	0.326	0.34	0.337	0.35	0.23	0.24
Biogenic volatile organic compounds released:	-0.028	-0.03	-0.394	-0.41	-1.157	-1.20	-2.752	-2.84	-4.827	-4.99	-7.235	-7.48	-9.825	-10.15	-12.819	-13.25	-4.88	-5.04
Avoided + net uptake	0.540	1.14	1.166	2.82	1.575	4.47	1.174	5.33	0.243	5.61	-1.083	5.42	-2.664	4.90	-4.613	4.05	-0.46	4.22
Hydrology (gal):																		
Rainfall interception	1,207	3.62	2,908	8.72	5,493	16.48	8,854	26.56	12,646	37.94	16,731	50.19	21,840	65.52	27,449	82.35	12,141	36.42
Aesthetics and other:																		
Yard		34.58		50.88		62.53		69.98		73.70		74.15		71.80		67.11		63.09
Public		39.18		57.66		70.86		79.30		83.52		84.03		81.37		76.05		71.50
Total benefits:																		
Yard: west		49.10		87.08		121.71		149.90		172.31		189.44		204.20		216.59		148.79
Yard: south		43.87		76.06		107.20		134.02		156.23		173.95		190.46		204.42		135.78
Yard: east		47.67		84.96		118.88		146.82		169.12		186.10		200.84		213.49		145.99
Public		46.11		74.97		101.70		124.94		144.40		160.36		175.21		188.30		127.00

Note: Annual values incorporate effects of tree loss. We assume that 5 percent of trees planted die during the first 5 years, 35 percent during the remaining 35 years, for a total mortality of 40 percent.

RU = resource unit.

[a] Values are the same for yard and public trees.

Table 13—Annual costs (dollars per tree) at 5-year intervals and 40-year average for a representative large tree (live oak)

Costs	Year 5	Year 10	Year 15	Year 20	Year 25	Year 30	Year 35	Year 40	40-year average
					Dollars				
Tree and planting:[a]									
Yard	88.00								11.00
Public	46.00								5.75
Pruning:									
Yard	0.07	1.26	1.18	4.37	4.03	3.69	3.34	3.00	2.42
Public	1.90	10.13	9.56	14.00	13.13	12.25	11.38	10.50	10.12
Remove and dispose:									
Yard	4.75	4.91	7.11	9.31	11.51	13.71	15.91	18.11	9.60
Public	1.79	3.25	4.70	6.16	7.61	9.06	10.52	11.97	6.27
Pest and disease:									
Yard	0.11	0.18	0.24	0.29	0.34	0.37	0.39	0.39	0.27
Public	0.11	0.19	0.26	0.32	0.38	0.42	0.45	0.47	0.30
Infrastructure repair:									
Yard	0.10	0.17	0.23	0.27	0.31	0.34	0.36	0.37	0.25
Public	0.84	1.43	1.96	2.41	2.80	3.11	3.35	3.52	2.26
Irrigation:									
Yard	0	0	0	0	0	0	0	0	0
Public	0	1.90	0	0	0	0	0	0	0.24
Cleanup:									
Yard	0.05	0.08	0.11	0.13	0.15	0.16	0.17	0.17	0.12
Public	0.39	0.68	0.92	1.14	1.32	1.47	1.58	1.66	1.07
Liability and legal:									
Yard	0.01	0.02	0.02	0.03	0.03	0.04	0.04	0.04	0.03
Public	0.09	0.15	0.21	0.26	0.30	0.33	0.36	0.38	0.24
Admin/inspect/other:									
Yard	0.64	1.08	1.46	1.77	2.01	2.20	2.31	2.25	1.62
Public	1.57	2.69	3.68	4.53	5.25	5.84	6.29	6.61	4.25
Total costs:									
Yard	93.72	7.70	10.35	16.18	18.38	20.50	22.52	24.33	25.31
Public	54.59	18.52	21.30	28.82	30.78	32.48	33.92	35.11	30.52

Note: Annual values incorporate effects of tree loss. We assume that 5 percent of trees planted die during the first 5 years, 35 percent during the remaining 35 years, for a total mortality of 40 percent.
[a] Although tree and planting costs occur in year 1, this value was divided by 5 years to derive an average annual cost for the first 5-year period.

Table 14—Annual net benefits (dollars per tree) at 5-year intervals and 40-year average for a representative large tree (live oak)

Total net benefits	Year 5	Year 10	Year 15	Year 20	Year 25	Year 30	Year 35	Year 40	40-year average
					Dollars				
Yard: west	-45	79	111	134	154	169	182	192	123
Yard: south	-50	68	97	118	138	153	168	180	110
Yard: east	-46	77	109	131	151	166	178	189	121
Public	-8	56	80	96	114	128	141	153	96

Note: Annual values incorporate effects of tree loss. We assume that 5 percent of trees planted die during the first 5 years, 35 percent during the remaining 35 years, for a total mortality of 40 percent.
See table 12 for annual benefits and table 13 for annual costs.

Table 15—Annual benefits (dollars per tree) at 5-year intervals and 40-year average for a representative conifer tree (slash pine)

Benefits/tree	Year 5 RU	Year 5 Value (Dollars)	Year 10 RU	Year 10 Value (Dollars)	Year 15 RU	Year 15 Value (Dollars)	Year 20 RU	Year 20 Value (Dollars)	Year 25 RU	Year 25 Value (Dollars)	Year 30 RU	Year 30 Value (Dollars)	Year 35 RU	Year 35 Value (Dollars)	Year 40 RU	Year 40 Value (Dollars)	40-year average RU	40-year average Value (Dollars)
Cooling (kWh):																		
Yard: west	8	1.05	18	2.37	28	3.72	37	4.89	40	5.23	42	5.48	43	5.68	44	5.82	32	4.28
Yard: south	8	1.05	18	2.37	28	3.72	37	4.89	40	5.23	42	5.48	43	5.68	44	5.82	32	4.28
Yard: east	8	1.05	18	2.37	28	3.72	37	4.89	40	5.23	42	5.48	43	5.68	44	5.82	32	4.28
Public	8	1.05	18	2.37	28	3.72	37	4.89	40	5.23	42	5.48	43	5.68	44	5.82	32	4.28
Heating (kBtu):																		
Yard: west	17	0.05	30	0.08	39	0.10	46	0.12	48	0.13	48	0.13	48	0.13	48	0.13	40	0.11
Yard: south	17	0.05	30	0.08	39	0.10	46	0.12	48	0.13	48	0.13	48	0.13	48	0.13	40	0.11
Yard: east	17	0.05	30	0.08	39	0.10	46	0.12	48	0.13	48	0.13	48	0.13	48	0.13	40	0.11
Public	17	0.05	30	0.08	39	0.10	46	0.12	48	0.13	48	0.13	48	0.13	48	0.13	40	0.11
Net energy (kBtu):																		
Yard: west	97	1.09	210	2.45	321	3.82	417	5.01	444	5.35	464	5.61	479	5.80	489	5.95	365	4.39
Yard: south	97	1.09	210	2.45	321	3.82	417	5.01	444	5.35	464	5.61	479	5.80	489	5.95	365	4.39
Yard: east	97	1.09	210	2.45	321	3.82	417	5.01	444	5.35	464	5.61	479	5.80	489	5.95	365	4.39
Public	97	1.09	210	2.45	321	3.82	417	5.01	444	5.35	464	5.61	479	5.80	489	5.95	365	4.39
Net carbon dioxide (lb):																		
Yard: west	34	0.11	79	0.26	146	0.49	195	0.65	190	0.64	184	0.62	183	0.61	199	0.67	151	0.51
Yard: south	34	0.11	79	0.26	146	0.49	195	0.65	190	0.64	184	0.62	183	0.61	199	0.67	151	0.51
Yard: east	34	0.11	79	0.26	146	0.49	195	0.65	190	0.64	184	0.62	183	0.61	199	0.67	151	0.51
Public	34	0.11	79	0.26	146	0.49	195	0.65	190	0.64	184	0.62	183	0.61	199	0.67	151	0.51
Air pollution (lb):[a]																		
Ozone uptake	0.1131	0.25	0.3049	0.67	0.5028	1.10	0.7001	1.54	0.8013	1.76	0.9026	1.98	1.0034	2.20	1.1031	2.42	0.68	1.49
Nitrous oxide uptake + avoided	0.0331	0.07	0.0778	0.17	0.1232	0.27	0.1645	0.36	0.1799	0.40	0.1936	0.43	0.2057	0.45	0.2166	0.48	0.15	0.33
Sulfur dioxide uptake + avoided	0.0193	0.04	0.0442	0.09	0.0696	0.14	0.0919	0.18	0.0989	0.20	0.1045	0.21	0.1090	0.22	0.1126	0.23	0.08	0.16
Small particulate matter uptake + avoided	0.0136	0.03	0.0485	0.10	0.1311	0.28	0.2507	0.53	0.3597	0.76	0.4666	0.98	0.5641	1.18	0.6711	1.41	0.31	0.66
Volatile organic compounds avoided	0.0079	0.01	0.0179	0.02	0.0280	0.03	0.0367	0.04	0.0393	0.04	0.0412	0.04	0.0426	0.04	0.0437	0.05	0.03	0.03
Biogenic volatile organic compounds released:	-0.001	0.00	-0.002	0.00	-0.010	-0.01	-0.028	-0.03	-0.054	-0.06	-0.088	-0.09	-0.128	-0.13	-0.181	-0.19	-0.06	-0.06
Avoided + net uptake:	0.186	0.40	0.491	1.05	0.845	1.81	1.216	2.62	1.425	3.09	1.620	3.55	1.797	3.97	1.966	4.39	1.19	2.61
Hydrology (gal):																		
Rainfall interception	234	0.70	751	2.25	1,645	4.94	2,711	8.13	3,510	10.53	4,309	12.93	5,192	15.58	6,317	18.95	3,084	9.25
Aesthetics and other:																		
Yard		10.06		16.90		22.94		13.07		13.69		14.13		14.38		14.46		14.95
Public		11.41		19.15		26.00		14.81		15.15		16.01		16.30		16.38		16.95
Total benefits:																		
Yard: west		12.37		22.91		34.00		29.48		33.30		36.83		40.35		44.41		31.71
Yard: south		12.37		22.91		34.00		29.48		33.30		36.83		40.35		44.41		31.71
Yard: east		12.37		22.91		34.00		29.48		33.30		36.83		40.35		44.41		31.71
Public		13.71		25.16		37.05		31.22		35.13		38.71		42.26		46.34		33.70

Note: Annual values incorporate effects of tree loss. We assume that 5 percent of trees planted die during the first 5 years, 35 percent during the remaining 35 years, for a total mortality of 40 percent.
RU = resource unit.
[a] Values are the same for yard and public trees.

Table 16—Annual costs (dollars per tree) at 5-year intervals and 40-year average for a representative conifer tree (slash pine)

Costs	Year 5	Year 10	Year 15	Year 20	Year 25	Year 30	Year 35	Year 40	40-year average
					Dollars				
Tree and planting:[a]									
Yard	88.00								11.00
Public	46.00								5.75
Pruning:									
Yard	0.07	1.26	1.18	4.37	4.03	3.69	3.34	3.00	2.71
Public	1.90	10.13	9.56	14.00	13.13	12.25	11.38	10.50	10.63
Remove and dispose:									
Yard	4.75	4.53	6.54	8.17	9.13	10.09	11.05	12.01	7.56
Public	1.79	2.99	4.32	5.40	6.03	6.67	7.31	7.94	4.92
Pest and disease:									
Yard	0.11	0.17	0.22	0.26	0.27	0.27	0.27	0.26	0.22
Public	0.11	0.18	0.24	0.28	0.30	0.31	0.31	0.31	0.24
Infrastructure repair:									
Yard	0.10	0.15	0.21	0.24	0.25	0.25	0.25	0.24	0.20
Public	0.84	1.32	1.80	2.12	2.22	2.29	2.33	2.33	1.80
Irrigation:									
Yard	0	0	0	0	0	0	0	0	0
Public	0	1.90	0	0	0	0	0	0	0.24
Cleanup:									
Yard	0.05	0.07	0.10	0.11	0.12	0.12	0.12	0.11	0.09
Public	0.39	0.62	0.85	1.00	1.05	1.08	1.10	1.10	0.85
Liability and legal:									
Yard	0.01	0.02	0.02	0.03	0.03	0.03	0.03	0.03	0.02
Public	0.09	0.14	0.19	0.23	0.24	0.25	0.25	0.25	0.19
Admin/inspect/other:									
Yard	0.64	0.99	1.34	1.55	1.60	1.62	1.60	2.25	1.29
Public	1.57	0.83	1.93	2.27	2.38	2.45	2.50	2.50	1.93
Total costs:									
Yard	93.72	7.20	9.61	14.73	15.41	16.06	16.66	17.91	23.10
Public	54.59	16.21	18.90	25.29	25.34	25.29	25.16	24.94	26.55

Note: Annual values incorporate effects of tree loss. We assume that 5 percent of trees planted die during the first 5 years, 35 percent during the remaining 35 years, for a total mortality of 40 percent.
[a] Although tree and planting costs occur in year 1, this value was divided by 5 years to derive an average annual cost for the first 5-year period.

Table 17—Annual net benefits (dollars per tree) at 5-year intervals and 40-year average for a representative conifer tree (slash pine)

Total net benefits	Year 5	Year 10	Year 15	Year 20	Year 25	Year 30	Year 35	Year 40	40-year average
					Dollars				
Yard: west	-81	16	24	15	18	21	24	27	9
Yard: south	-81	16	24	15	18	21	24	27	9
Yard: east	-81	16	24	15	18	21	24	27	9
Public	-41	9	18	6	10	13	17	21	7

Note: Annual values incorporate effects of tree loss. We assume that 5 percent of trees planted die during the first 5 years, 35 percent during the remaining 35 years, for a total mortality of 40 percent.
See table 15 for annual benefits and table 16 for annual costs.

Appendix 3: Procedures for Estimating Benefits and Costs

Approach
Pricing Benefits and Costs

In this study, annual benefits and costs over a 40-year planning horizon were estimated for newly planted trees in three residential yard locations (east, south, and west of the dwelling unit) and a public streetside or park location. Trees in these hypothetical locations are called "yard" and "public" trees, respectively. Prices were assigned to each cost (e.g., planting, pruning, removal, irrigation, infrastructure repair, liability) and benefit (e.g., heating/cooling energy savings, air-pollution reduction, stormwater-runoff reduction) through direct estimation and implied valuation of benefits as environmental externalities. This approach made it possible to estimate the net benefits of plantings in "typical" locations with "typical" tree species.

To account for differences in the mature size and growth rates of different tree species, we report results for small, medium, and large broadleaf trees and a conifer. Results are reported for 5-year intervals for 40 years.

Mature tree height is frequently used to characterize a tree as being a small, medium, or large species because matching tree height to available overhead space is an important design consideration. However, in this analysis, leaf surface area (**LSA**) and crown diameter were also used to characterize **mature tree size**. These additional measurements are useful indicators for many functional benefits of trees that relate to leaf-atmosphere processes (e.g., interception, transpiration, photosynthesis). Tree growth rates, dimensions, and LSA estimates are based on tree growth modeling.

Growth Modeling

Growth models are based on data collected in Orlando, Florida. Using Orlando's street tree inventory that included 68,211 trees, we measured a stratified random sample of 20 of the most common tree species to establish relations between tree age, size, leaf area, and biomass. The species were as follows:

* American sycamore (*Platanus occidentalis* L.)
* Camphor (*Cinnamomum camphora* (L.) J. Presl.)
* Carolina laurelcherry (*Prunus caroliniana* (Mill.) Aiton.)
* Chinese elm (*Ulmus parvifolia* Jacq.)
* Chinese tallow (*Triadica sebifera* (L.) Small)

103

- Common crapemyrtle (*Lagerstroemia indica* L.)
- Golden raintree (*Koelreuteria elegans* (Seem.) A.C. Sm.)
- Laurel oak (*Quercus laurifolia* Michx.)
- Live oak (*Quercus virginiana* Mill.)
- Loquat tree (*Eriobotrya japonica* (Thunb.) Lindl.)
- Oriental arborvitae (*Platycladus orientalis* (L.) Franco)
- Queen palm (*Syagrus romanzoffiana* (Cham.) Glassman)
- Red maple (*Acer rubrum* L.)
- Sabal palm (*Sabal palm* (Walt.) Lodd. ex J.A. & J.H. Schultes)
- Slash pine (*Pinus elliottii* Engelm.)
- Southern magnolia (*Magnolia grandiflora* L.)
- Southern redcedar (*Juniperus virginiana* var. *silicicola* (Small) E. Murray)
- Sweetgum (*Liquidambar styraciflua* L.)
- Washington fan palm (*Washingtonia robusta* H. Wendl.)

For the growth models, information spanning the life cycle of predominant tree species was collected. The inventory was stratified into the following nine **diameter-at-breast height** (d.b.h.) classes:

- 0 to 2.9 in
- 3.0 to 5.9 in
- 6.0 to 11.9 in
- 12.0 to 17.9 in
- 18.0 to 23.9 in
- 24.0 to 29.9 in
- 30.0 to 35.9 in
- 36.0 to 41.9 in
- >42.0 in

Thirty-five to sixty trees of each species were randomly selected for surveying, along with an equal number of alternative trees. Tree measurements included d.b.h. (to nearest 0.1 cm [0.04 in] by sonar measuring device), tree crown and bole height (to nearest 0.5 m [1.6 ft] by clinometer), crown diameter in two directions (parallel and perpendicular to nearest street to nearest 0.5 m [1.6 ft] by sonar measuring device), and tree condition and location. Replacement trees were sampled when trees from the original sample population could not be located. Tree age was determined by street-tree managers using a variety of methods including ring counts on removed trees, planting records, development dates, historical documents, and resident interviews. Field work was conducted in June and July 2008.

Crown volume and leaf area were estimated from computer processing of tree-crown images obtained with a digital camera. The method has shown greater accuracy than other techniques (± 20 percent of actual leaf area) in estimating crown volume and leaf area of open-grown trees (Peper and McPherson 2003).

Segmented linear regression was used to fit predictive models with d.b.h. as a function of age for each of the 20 sampled species. Predictions of LSA, crown diameter, and height metrics were modeled as a function of d.b.h. by using best-fit models. After inspecting the growth curves for each species, we selected the typical small, medium, and large tree species for this report.

Reporting Results

Results are reported in terms of annual values per tree planted. However, to make these calculations realistic, mortality rates are included. Based on our survey of regional municipal foresters and commercial arborists, this analysis assumed that 40 percent of the hypothetical planted trees died over the 40-year period. Annual mortality rates were 1.0 percent. The accounting approach "grows" trees in different locations and uses computer simulation to directly calculate the annual flow of benefits and costs as trees mature and die (McPherson 1992).

Benefits and costs are directly connected with tree-size variables such as trunk d.b.h., tree canopy cover, and LSA. For instance, pruning and removal costs usually increase with tree size, expressed as d.b.h. For some parameters, such as sidewalk repair, costs are negligible for young trees but increase relatively rapidly as tree roots grow large enough to heave pavement. For other parameters, such as air-pollutant uptake and rainfall interception, benefits are related to tree canopy cover and leaf area.

Most benefits occur on an annual basis, but some costs are periodic. For instance, street trees may be pruned on regular cycles but are removed in a less regular fashion (e.g., when they pose a hazard or soon after they die). In this analysis, most costs and benefits are reported for the year in which they occur. However, periodic costs such as pruning, pest and disease control, and infrastructure repair are presented on an average annual basis. Although spreading one-time costs over each year of a maintenance cycle does not alter the 40-year nominal expenditure, it can lead to inaccuracies if future costs are discounted to the present.

Benefit and Cost Valuation

Source of cost estimates—

Frequency and costs of public tree management were estimated based on surveys with municipal foresters in Brooksville, Dunedin, Orlando, St. Petersburg, and Lakeland, Florida. Commercial arborists from Plantation, Umatilla, and Parrish,

Florida, who work throughout Central Florida, provided information on tree management costs on residential properties.

Monetizing benefits—

To monetize effects of trees on energy use, we take the perspective of a residential customer by using retail electricity and natural gas prices for utilities serving Central Florida. The retail price of energy reflects a full accounting of costs as paid by the end user, such as the utility costs of power generation, transmission, distribution, administration, marketing, and profit. This perspective aligns with our modeling method, which calculates energy effects of trees based on differences among consumers in heating and air conditioning equipment types, saturations, building construction types, and base loads.

The preferred way to value air quality benefits from trees is to first determine the costs of damages to human health from polluted air, then calculate the value of avoided costs because trees are cleaning the air. Economic valuation of damages to human health usually uses information on willingness to pay to avoid damages obtained via interviews or direct estimates of the monetary costs of damages (e.g., alleviating headaches, extending life). Empirical correlations developed by Wang and Santini (1995) reviewed five studies and 15 sets of regional cost data to relate per-ton costs of various pollutant emissions to regional ambient air quality measurements and population size. We use their damage-based estimates unless the values are negative, in which case we use their control-cost-based estimates.

Calculating Benefits

Calculating Energy Benefits

The prototypical building used as a basis for the simulations was typical of post-1980 construction practices, and represents approximately one-third of the total single-family residential housing stock in the Central Florida region. The house was a one-story brick building on a slab with total conditioned floor area of 1,620 ft^2, window area (single-glazed) of 264 ft^2, and wall and ceiling insulation of R11 and R19, respectively. The central cooling system had a **seasonal energy efficiency ratio** (SEER) of 10, and the natural gas furnace had an **annual fuel utilization efficiency (AFUE)** of 78 percent. Building footprints were square, reflecting average impacts for a large number of buildings (McPherson and Simpson 1999). Buildings were simulated with 1.5-ft overhangs. Blinds had a visual density of 37 percent and were assumed to be closed when the air conditioner was operating. Summer thermostat settings were 78 °F; winter settings were 68 °F during the day and 60 °F at night. Because the prototype building was larger, but more energy efficient, than most other construction types, our projected energy savings can be considered similar to those for older, less thermally efficient, but smaller buildings. The energy simulations relied on typical meteorological year (TMY2) weather data from Orlando (National Oceanic and Atmospheric Administration 2007).

Calculating energy savings—

Dollar values for energy savings were based on electricity and natural gas prices of $0.132/kWh (Orlando Utilities Commission 2009) and $0.268/therm (Peoples Gas 2009), respectively. Homes were assumed to have central air conditioning and natural gas heating.

Calculating shade effects—

Residential yard trees were within 60 ft of homes so as to directly shade walls and windows. Shade effects of these trees on building energy use were simulated for small, medium, and large broadleaf trees and a conifer at three tree-to-building distances, following methods outlined by McPherson and Simpson (1999). The small tree (common crapemyrtle) had a visual density of 70 percent during summer and 25 percent during winter. The medium tree (southern magnolia) had a density of 21 percent during summer and winter. The large tree (live oak) had a visual density of 15 percent during summer and winter, and the conifer (slash pine) had a density of 10 percent year round. Crown densities for calculating shade were based on published values where available (Hammond et al. 1980, McPherson 1984).

Foliation periods for deciduous trees were obtained from the literature (Hammond et al. 1980, McPherson 1984) and adjusted for the region's climate based on consultation with the forestry manager (Kittsley 2009). Small trees were leafless January 1 through March 31; medium and large broadleaf trees and conifers were evergreen. Results of shade effects for each tree were averaged over distance and weighted by occurrence within each of three distance classes: 28 percent at 10 to 20 ft, 68 percent at 20 to 40 ft, and 4 percent at 40 to 60 ft (McPherson and Simpson 1999). Results are reported for trees shading east-, south-, and west-facing surfaces. The conifer is included as a windbreak tree located greater than 50 ft from the residence so it does not shade the building. Our results for public trees are conservative in that we assumed that they do not provide shading benefits. For example, in Modesto, California, 15 percent of total annual dollar energy savings from street trees was due to shade and 85 percent due to climate effects (McPherson et al. 1999a).

Calculating climate effects—

In addition to localized shade effects, which were assumed to accrue only to residential yard trees, lowered air temperatures and windspeeds from increased neighborhood tree cover (referred to as climate effects) produced a net decrease in demand for winter heating and summer cooling (reduced windspeeds by themselves may increase or decrease cooling demand, depending on the circumstances). Climate effects on energy use, air temperature, and windspeed, as a function of neighborhood canopy cover, were estimated from published values (McPherson and Simpson 1999). Existing tree canopy cover for Orlando was 18 percent based on estimates of urban tree cover for Florida (Nowak and Crane 2002); building cover was estimated to be 25 percent. Canopy cover was calculated to increase by 4.5, 6.8, 14.2 and 6.0 percent for 20-year-old small, medium, and large broadleaf trees and the conifer, respectively, based on an effective lot size (actual lot size plus a portion of adjacent street and other rights-of-way) of 10,000 ft^2, and one tree on average was assumed per lot. Climate effects were estimated by simulating effects of air temperature and wind reductions on energy use. Climate effects accrued for both public and yard trees.

Calculating windbreak effects—
Trees near buildings result in additional windspeed reductions beyond those from the aggregate effects of trees throughout the neighborhood. This leads to a small additional reduction in annual heating energy use of about 2 percent per tree for conifers in the Gulf Coast region (McPherson and Simpson 1999). Yard and public conifer trees were assumed to be windbreaks, and therefore located where they did not increase heating loads by obstructing winter sun. Windbreak effects were not attributed to deciduous trees because their crowns are leafless during winter and do not block winds near ground level.

Atmospheric Carbon Dioxide Reduction

Calculating reduction in carbon dioxide emissions from powerplants—
Conserving energy in buildings can reduce carbon dioxide (CO_2) emissions from powerplants. These emission reductions were calculated as the product of energy savings for heating and cooling based on CO_2 **emission factors** (table 18) and were based on data for the Orlando Metropolitan region where the average fuel mix is 97.9 percent coal, 1.8 percent biomass, and less than 1 percent natural gas and oil (US EPA 2006b). The value of $0.00334 per pound of CO_2 reduction (table 18) was based on the average value in Pearce (2003).

Calculating carbon storage—
Sequestration, the net rate of CO_2 storage in above- and belowground biomass over the course of one growing season, was calculated by using tree height and d.b.h.

growth estimates from the Orlando, Florida, street tree sample with volume equations for urban, open-grown trees growing in a temperate climate zone (McHale et al. 2009, Pillsbury et al. 1998). Volume estimates were converted to dry-weight estimates using density factors based on same species or nearest taxonomic relationship (Markwardt 1930) and divided by 78 percent to incorporate root biomass. Dry-weight biomass was converted to carbon (50 percent), and these values were converted to CO_2. The amount of CO_2 sequestered each year is the annual increment of CO_2 stored as biomass each year.

Calculating CO_2 released by power equipment—
Tree-related emissions of CO_2, based on gasoline and diesel fuel consumption during tree care in our survey cities, were calculated by using the value 0.34 lb CO_2/in d.b.h. This amount may overestimate CO_2 release for less intensively maintained residential yard trees.

Calculating CO_2 released during decomposition—
To calculate CO_2 released through decomposition of dead woody biomass, we conservatively estimated that dead trees were removed and mulched in the year that death occurred, and that 80 percent of their stored carbon was released to the atmosphere as CO_2 in the same year (McPherson and Simpson 1999).

Calculating Reduction in Air Pollutant Emissions

Reductions in building energy use also result in reduced emission of air pollutants from powerplants and space-heating equipment. Volatile organic hydrocarbons (VOCs) and nitrogen dioxide (NO_2)—precursors of ozone (O_3) formation—as well as sulfur dioxide (SO_2) and particulate matter of <10 micron diameter (PM_{10}) were considered. Changes in average annual emissions and their monetary values were calculated in the same way as for CO_2, with utility-specific emissions factors for electricity (Ottinger et al. 1990, US EPA 2006a). The price of emissions savings was derived from models that calculate the marginal cost of controlling different pollutants to meet air quality standards (Wang and Santini 1995). Emissions concentrations were obtained from U.S. EPA (2006b) (table 18), and population estimates from the U.S. Census Bureau (2009).

Calculating pollutant uptake by trees—
Trees also remove pollutants from the atmosphere. The modeling method we applied was developed by Scott et al. (1998). It calculates **hourly pollutant dry deposition** per tree expressed as the product of deposition velocity ($V_d = 1 \div [R_a + R_b + R_c]$), pollutant concentration (C), canopy-projection area (CP), and a time step, where R_a, R_b, and R_c are aerodynamic, boundary layer, and stomatal resistances.

Table 18—Emissions factors and implied values for carbon dioxide and criteria air pollutants

Emission factor	Electricity[a]	Natural gas[b]	Implied value[c]
	Pounds per megawatt hour	*Pounds per million British thermal units*	*Dollars per pound*
Carbon dioxide	2,037	118	0.00334
Nitrous oxide	2.808	0.1020	2.20
Sulfur dioxide	2.257	0.0006	2.01
Small particulate matter	0.985	0.0075	2.10
Volatile organic compounds	0.984	0.0054	1.03

[a] U.S. EPA 2006b, except Ottinger et al. 1990 for volatile organic compounds.
[b] U.S. EPA 1998.
[c] Carbon dioxide from Pearce 2003. Value for others based on methods of Wang and Santini (1995) using emissions concentrations from U.S. EPA (2006b) and population estimates from the U.S. Census Bureau (2009).

Hourly deposition velocities for each pollutant were calculated during the growing season by using estimates for the resistances ($R_a + R_b + R_c$) for each hour throughout the year. Hourly concentrations for 2007 were selected as representative for modeling deposition based on a review of mean PM_{10} and O_3 concentrations for the years 2000–2008. The O_3, NO_2, SO_2, and PM_{10} data were from Winter Park (Kruger 2009). Hourly air temperature, solar radiation, and windspeed data were obtained for the Apopka weather station of the Florida Automated Weather Network (Florida Automated Weather Network 2009). To set a value for pollutant uptake by trees, we used the procedure described above for emissions reductions (table 18). The monetary value for NO_2 was used for O_3.

Estimating biogenic volatile organic compounds emissions from trees—
Annual emissions for biogenic volatile organic compounds (BVOCs) were estimated for the three tree species by using the algorithms of Guenther et al. (1991, 1993). Annual emissions were simulated during the growing season over 40 years. The emission of carbon as isoprene was expressed as a product of the base emission rate (micrograms of carbon per gram of dry foliar biomass per hour), adjusted for sunlight and temperature and the amount of dry, foliar biomass present in the tree. Monoterpene emissions were estimated by using a base emission rate adjusted for temperature. The base emission rates for the four species were based on values reported in the literature (Benjamin and Winer 1998). Hourly emissions were summed to get monthly and annual emissions.

Annual dry foliar biomass was derived from field data collected in Orlando during the summer of 2008. The amount of foliar biomass present for each year of the simulated tree's life was unique for each species. Hourly air temperature and solar radiation data for 2007 described in the pollutant uptake section were used as model inputs.

Calculating net air quality benefits—

Net air quality benefits were calculated by subtracting the costs associated with BVOC emissions from benefits associated with pollutant uptake and avoided power-plant emissions. The o_3-reduction benefit from lowering summertime air temperatures, thereby reducing hydrocarbon emissions from **anthropogenic** and **biogenic** sources, was estimated as a function of canopy cover following McPherson and Simpson (1999). They used peak summer air temperature reductions of 0.1 °F for each percentage increase in canopy cover. Hourly changes in air temperature were calculated by reducing this peak air temperature at every hour based on hourly maximum and minimum temperature for that day, scaled by magnitude of maximum total global solar radiation for each day relative to the maximum value for the year.

Stormwater Benefits

Estimating rainfall interception by tree canopies—

A numerical simulation model was used to estimate annual rainfall interception (Xiao et al. 2000). The interception model accounted for water intercepted by the tree, as well as throughfall and **stem flow**. Intercepted water is stored temporarily on canopy leaf and bark surfaces. Rainwater drips from leaf surfaces, flows down the stem surface to the ground, or evaporates. Tree-canopy parameters that affect interception include species, leaf and stem surface areas, **shade coefficients** (visual density of the crown), foliation periods, and tree dimensions (e.g., tree height, crown height, crown diameter, and d.b.h.). Windspeeds were estimated for different heights above the ground; from this, rates of evaporation were estimated.

The volume of water stored in the tree crown was calculated from crown-projection area (area under tree dripline), **leaf area indices** (**LAI**, the ratio of LSA to crown projection area), and the depth of water captured by the canopy surface. Gap fractions, foliation periods, and **tree surface saturation storage capacity** influence the amount of projected throughfall. Tree surface saturation was 1.0 mm (0.04 in) for all trees.

Hourly meteorological and rainfall data for 2008 from the Orlando International Airport (ORL) (Latitude: 28.43°, Longitude: -81.33°, Elevation: 27.4 m (96 ft) above sea level, National Oceanic and Atmospheric Administration/National Weather Service COOPID: 086628) in Orlando, Florida, were used in this simulation. Annual precipitation during 2008 was 53.8 in, which is slightly higher than long-time annual average precipitation 48.35 in (1228.1 mm). The year 2008 was chosen because, although the overall amount of rainfall was higher, it most closely approximated the monthly distribution of the long-term average rainfall. Storm events less than 0.1 in (2.5 mm) were assumed to not produce runoff and were dropped from the analysis. More complete descriptions of the interception model can be found in Xiao et al. (1998, 2000).

Calculating water quality protection and flood control benefit—
The benefits that result from reduced surface runoff include reduced property damage from flooding and reduced loss of soil and habitat owing to erosion and sediment flow. Reduced runoff also results in improved water quality in streams, lakes, and rivers. This can translate into improved aquatic habitats, less human disease and illness owing to contact with contaminated water and reduced stormwater treatment costs.

The city of Orlando spends approximately $36.5 million annually on operations and maintenance of its stormwater management system (McCann 2009). To calculate annual runoff, the USDA Soil Conservation Service TR55 (USDA SCS 1986) calculations were used and curve numbers were assigned for each land use. Land use percentages were obtained from the city's parcel geographic information system (GIS) layers (2009). We calculated runoff depth for each land use (12.4 in, citywide) and found the citywide total to be 37,374 acre-feet. The annual stormwater control cost was estimated to be $0.0019 per gallon of runoff.

Aesthetic and Other Benefits

Many benefits attributed to urban trees are difficult to translate into economic terms. Beautification, privacy, wildlife habitat, shade that increases human comfort, sense of place and well-being are services that are difficult to price. However, the value of some of these benefits may be captured in the property values of the land on which trees stand.

To estimate the value of these "other" benefits, we applied results of research that compared differences in sales prices of houses to statistically quantify the difference associated with trees. All else being equal, the difference in sales price reflects the willingness of buyers to pay for the benefits and costs associated with trees. This approach has the virtue of capturing in the sales price both the benefits and costs of trees as perceived by the buyers. Limitations to this approach include difficulty determining the value of individual trees on a property, the need to extrapolate results from studies done years ago in other parts of the country, and the need to extrapolate results from front-yard trees on residential properties to trees in other locations (e.g., back yards, streets, parks, and nonresidential land).

A large tree adds value to a home—

Anderson and Cordell (1988) surveyed 844 single-family residences in Athens, Georgia, and found that each large front-yard tree was associated with a 0.88 percent increase in the average home sales price. This percentage of sales price was used as an indicator of the additional value a resident in the Central Florida region would gain from selling a home with a large tree.

We averaged the home prices for the Orlando ($223,500), Cape Coral/Fort Myers ($178,100), Deltona/Daytona Beach/Ormand Beach ($173,400), Ocala ($147,600), Palm Bay/Melbourne/Titusville ($148,000), Sarasota/Bradenton/Venice ($266,400), and Tampa/St. Petersburg/Clearwater ($180,800) metropolitan statistical areas as our starting point ($195,633; National Association of Realtors 2009). Therefore, the value of a large tree that added 0.88 percent to the sales price of such a home was $1,722. To estimate annual benefits, the total added value was divided by the LSA of a 40-year-old live oak ($1,722 per 3,801 ft^2) to yield the base value of LSA, $0.45 per ft^2. This value was multiplied by the amount of LSA added to the tree during 1 year of growth.

Additionally, not all street trees are as effective as front-yard trees in increasing property values. For example, trees adjacent to multifamily housing units will not increase the property value at the same rate as trees in front of single-family homes (Gonzales 2004). Therefore, a citywide street tree reduction factor (0.83) was applied to prorate trees' value based on the assumption that trees adjacent to different land uses make different contributions to property sales prices. For this analysis, the street reduction factor reflects the distribution of street trees in Honolulu by land use. Reduction factors were single-home residential (100 percent), multihome residential (70 percent), small commercial (66 percent), industrial/institutional/large commercial (40 percent), park/vacant/other (40 percent) (Gonzales 2004, McPherson 2001).

Calculating the aesthetic and other benefits of residential yard trees—

To calculate the base value for a large tree on private residential property we assumed that a 40-year-old live oak in the front yard increased the property sales price by $1,722. Approximately 75 percent of all yard trees, however, are in back yards (Richards et al. 1984). Lacking specific research findings, it was assumed that back-yard trees had 75 percent of the impact on "curb appeal" and sales price compared to front-yard trees. The average annual aesthetic and other benefits for a tree on private property were, therefore, estimated as $0.60 per square foot of LSA. To estimate annual benefits, this value was multiplied by the amount of LSA added to the tree during 1 year of growth.

Calculating the aesthetic value of a public tree—

The base value of street trees was calculated in the same way as yard trees. However, because street trees may be adjacent to land with little resale potential, an adjusted value was calculated. An analysis of street trees in Modesto, California, sampled from aerial photographs (sample size 8 percent of street trees), found that 15 percent were located adjacent to nonresidential or commercial property (McPherson et al. 1999a). We assumed that 33 percent of these trees—or 5 percent of the entire street-tree population—produced no benefits associated with property value increases. Although the impact of parks on real estate values has been reported (Hammer et al. 1974, Schroeder 1982, Tyrvainen 1999), to our knowledge, the onsite and external benefits of park trees alone have not been isolated (More et al. 1988). After reviewing the literature and recognizing an absence of data, we made the conservative estimate that park trees had half the impact on property prices of street trees.

Given these assumptions, typical large street and park trees were estimated to increase property values by $0.74 and $0.44 per square foot of LSA, respectively. Assuming that 80 percent of all municipal trees were on streets and 20 percent in parks, a weighted average benefit of $0.68 per square foot of LSA was calculated for each tree.

Calculating Costs

Tree management costs were estimated based on surveys with municipal foresters in Brooksville, Dunedin, Orlando, St. Petersburg, and Lakeland, Florida. In addition, several commercial arborists from Plantation, Umatilla, and Parrish, Florida, who work throughout Central Florida, provided information on tree management costs on residential properties.

Planting

Planting costs include the cost of the tree and the cost for planting, staking, mulching, and establishment irrigation if necessary. Based on our survey of Central Florida municipal and commercial arborists, planting costs ranged widely from $125 for a 15-gal tree to $2,000 for very large trees. In this analysis, we assumed that a 3-in yard tree was planted at a cost of $440. The cost for planting a 2-in public tree was $230.

Pruning

Pruning costs for public trees—

After studying data from municipal forestry programs and their contractors, we assumed that young public trees were inspected and pruned once during the first 5 years after planting, at a cost of $10 per tree. Pruning for small trees (< 20 ft tall) cost $20 per tree on a 5-year cycle. More expensive equipment and more time were required to prune medium trees ($90 per tree) once every 8 years and large trees ($175 per tree) once every 10 years. After factoring in pruning frequency, annualized costs were $2, $4, $11.25, and $17.50 per tree for public young, small, medium, and large trees, respectively.

Pruning costs for yard trees—

Based on findings from our survey of commercial arborists in the Central Florida region, pruning cycles for yard trees were different than for public trees. Young trees (first 5 years after planting) were pruned once in the first 4 years, and small, medium, and large trees were pruned every 10 years. Only about 20 percent of all private trees, however, were professionally pruned (**contract rate**), although the number of professionally pruned trees grows as the trees grow. We assumed that professionals are paid to prune all large trees, 60 percent of the medium trees, and only 6 percent of the small and young trees and conifers (Summit and McPherson 1998). Using these contract rates, along with average pruning prices ($25, $20, $120, and $300 for young, small, medium, and large trees, respectively), the average annual costs for pruning a yard tree were $0.08, $0.02, $1.5, and $6.00 for young, small, medium, and large trees, respectively.

Tree and Stump Removal

The costs for tree removal and disposal were $30 per in d.b.h. for public trees, and $40 per in d.b.h. for yard trees. Stump removal costs were $4 per in d.b.h. for public trees and $5 per in d.b.h. for yard trees. Therefore, total costs for removal and disposal of trees and stumps were $34 per in d.b.h. for public trees, and $45 per in d.b.h. for yard trees. Removal costs of trees less than 3 inches in diameter were $50 and $68 for yard and public trees, respectively.

Pest and Disease Control

Expenditures for pest and disease control in the Central Florida region are minimal for public and yard trees. They averaged about $0.25 per tree per year or approximately $0.02/in d.b.h.

Irrigation Costs

Rain falls regularly throughout most of the region during summer and fall and additional irrigation is not usually needed after establishment when trees are planted into landscapes with installed irrigation. Costs during establishment were reported to be $0.25 per tree for both public and yard trees.

Other Costs for Public and Yard Trees

Other costs associated with the management of trees include expenditures for infrastructure repair/root pruning, leaf-litter cleanup, litigation/liability, and inspection/administration. Cost data were obtained from the municipal arborist survey and assume that 80 percent of public trees are street trees and 20 percent are park trees. Costs for park trees tend to be lower than for street trees because there are fewer conflicts with infrastructure such as power lines and sidewalks.

Infrastructure conflict costs—

As trees and sidewalks age, roots can cause damage to sidewalks, curbs, paving, and sewer lines. Sidewalk repair is typically one of the largest expenses for public trees (McPherson and Peper 1995). Infrastructure-related expenditures for public trees in Central Florida communities were approximately $2 per tree on an annual basis. Roots from most trees in yards do not damage sidewalks and sewers. Therefore, the cost for yard trees was estimated to be only 10 percent of the cost for public trees.

Litter and storm cleanup costs—

The average annual per-tree cost for litter cleanup (i.e., street sweeping, storm-damage cleanup) was $1.10/tree ($0.08/in d.b.h.). This value was based on average annual litter cleanup costs and storm cleanup, assuming a large storm results in extraordinary costs about twice a decade. Because most residential yard trees are not littering the streets with leaves, it was assumed that cleanup costs for yard trees were 10 percent of those for public trees.

Liability costs—

Urban trees can incur costly payments and legal fees owing to trip-and-fall claims. A survey of Western U.S. cities showed that an average of 8.8 percent of total tree-related expenditures was spent on tree-related liability (McPherson 2000). Communities in our survey report spending on average $0.25 per tree for tree-related liabilities annually.

Inspection and administration costs—
Municipal tree programs have administrative costs for salaries of supervisors and clerical staff, operating costs, and overhead. Our survey found that the average annual cost for inspection and administration associated with street- and park-tree management was $2 per tree ($0.18 per in d.b.h.). Trees on private property do not accrue this expense.

Calculating Net Benefits

Benefits Accrue at Different Scales

When calculating net benefits, it is important to recognize that trees produce benefits that accrue both on- and offsite. Benefits are realized at four scales: parcel, neighborhood, community, and global. For example, property owners with onsite trees not only benefit from increased property values, but they may also directly benefit from improved human health (e.g., reduced exposure to cancer-causing ultraviolet radiation) and greater psychological well-being through visual and direct contact with plants. However, on the cost side, increased health care costs owing to allergies and respiratory ailments related to pollen may be incurred because of nearby trees. We assume that these intangible benefits and costs are reflected in what we term "aesthetics and other benefits."

The property owner can obtain additional economic benefits from onsite trees depending on their location and condition. For example, carefully located onsite trees can provide air-conditioning savings by shading windows and walls and cooling building microclimates. This benefit can extend to adjacent neighbors who benefit from shade and air-temperature reductions that lower their cooling costs.

Neighborhood attractiveness and property values can be influenced by the extent of tree canopy cover on individual properties. At the community scale, benefits are realized through cleaner air and water, as well as social, educational, and employment and job training benefits that can reduce costs for health care, welfare, crime prevention, and other social service programs.

Reductions in atmospheric CO_2 concentrations owing to trees are an example of benefits that are realized at the global scale.

Annual benefits are calculated as:

$$B = E + AQ + CO_2 + H + A$$

where

E = value of net annual energy savings (cooling and heating)

AQ = value of annual air-quality improvement (pollutant uptake, avoided powerplant emissions, and BVOC emissions)

CO_2 = value of annual CO_2 reductions (sequestration, avoided emissions, release from tree care and decomposition)

H = value of annual stormwater-runoff reductions

A = value of annual aesthetics and other benefits

On the other side of the benefit-cost equation are costs for tree planting and management. Expenditures are borne by property owners (irrigation, pruning, and removal) and the community (pollen and other health care costs). Annual costs (C) are the sum of costs for residential yard trees (C_Y) and public trees (C_P) where:

$C_Y = P + T + R + D + I + S + Cl + L$

$C_P = P + T + R + D + I + S + Cl + L + A$

where

P = cost of tree and planting

T = average annual tree pruning cost

R = annualized tree and stump removal and disposal cost

D = average annual pest- and disease-control cost

I = annual irrigation cost

S = average annual cost to repair/mitigate infrastructure damage

Cl = annual litter and storm cleanup cost

L = average annual cost for litigation and settlements from tree-related claims

A = annual program administration, inspection, and other costs

Net benefits are calculated as the difference between total benefits and costs:

Net benefits = B - C

Benefit-cost ratios (BCR) are calculated as the ratio of benefits to costs:

BCR = $B \div C$